Walking Bridges Using Poetry as a Compass

Supporting the Divine

A kiss is a cantilever bridge—
Two lips meeting in the middle,
air jumping up and down
(vortices exciting the molecules);
tension and compression
at such an angle two hearts
can safely walk hope across
no matter how many miles
or old the ground.—SWW

Walking Bridges Using Poetry as a Compass

Poems about Bridges Real and Imagined by 70 Poets,
with Directions for Five Self-Guided Explorations

EDITED BY
SHARON WOOD WORTMAN
AND KIRSTEN RIAN
&
ILLUSTRATED BY
ED WORTMAN, P.E.

Urban Adventure Press
www.bridgestones.com   P.O. Box 3403 Portland, OR 97208-3403
Office (503) 222-5535 Cell (503) 330-0900

REGIONAL ARTS & CULTURE COUNCIL   This book is funded in part by the Regional Arts & Culture Council.

Urban Adventure Press

PO Box 3403

Portland, OR 97208-3403, U.S.A.

<www.bridgestories.com>

Published in 2007

Printed by Bridgetown Printing Co. in Portland, Oregon

Library of Congress Preassigned Control Number Data

Wood Wortman, Sharon, 1944–

Walking Bridges Using Poetry as a Compass: Poems about Bridges Real and Imagined by 70 Poets, with Directions for Five Self-Guided Explorations,

edited by Sharon Wood Wortman and Kirsten Rian. Illustrated by Ed Wortman, P.E.

First ed.

Includes bibliographical references and index.

ISBN-13: 978-0-9787365-3-8 (pbk.)

1. Walking—Portland—Guidebooks—Poetry. 2. Portland (Or.)—Guidebooks. 1. Title.

∞ The paper used in this publication meets the minimum requirements of the American National Standard for Information Sciences—Permanence of Paper for Printed Library Materials, ANSI Z39.48-1992.

Facts stated in the itineraries in this book are true to the best of the author's knowledge. Bus routes, business operations, and other specifics are subject to change without notice.

To the poets who design words
so we can stand the loads
this world hands us to carry

and

to the newcomer to Portland who might not at first see
that the bridges here, always moving around,
are like family members
with Attention Deficit Hyperactivity Disorder
and seldom boring.

"Thou therefore which teachest another, teachest thou not thyself?"
—Romans

Contents

I Main Span – 41 Poems by 41 Poets

II Beyond Local Piers – 14 Poems by 14 Poets

III Distant Approaches – 14 Poems by 14 Poets

Illustrations by Ed Wortman

Exploration One

Exploration Two

Exploration 5

Acknowledgments

Thanks are due to the publications in which these poems appeared: "Autumn," *The Oregonian* (Nov. 3, 2002); "Birds, Probably Birds," *Comstock Review* (Spring 2007); "Crossing Dark Water," *Broken Word: The Alberta Street Anthology*, Church of Poetry Press (April 2007); "Ghost Bridge," *Windfall: A Journal of Poetry of Place* (Spring 2003); "Ice Storm Paralyzes City," *Windfall: A Journal of Poetry of Place* (Spring 2003); "La Pine Middle Schoolers Encounter Sidewalk Weather," *Windfall: A Journal of Poetry of Place* (Fall 2007); "Maneuvers," *Willow Springs* (1986); "On The Willamette Bridge," *Verseweavers*, Oregon State Poetry Association (Spring 2006), also appeared in *Hipfish* (Nov/Dec 2006); "One Morning," *Manzanita Quarterly* under the title "Fantasy" (Winter 2000–2001); "Piercing One Ear," *Bridges: A Jewish Feminist Journal* (Spring 2006); "Poem for First-Year Teachers," *Portland Magazine* (forthcoming); "Soulspans," *Portland Magazine* (Winter 1992); "Supporting the Divine," *The Oregon Civil Engineer*, Newsletter of the American Society of Civil Engineers Oregon Section (October 2007); "That Sweet Portland Symphony" (excerpt), *Portland Tribune* (Sept. 21, 2007); "Wherever I come to it," *Bridges* (Fall 2007); "White Birds," *Verseweavers*, Oregon State Poetry Association (Spring 2006).

These poems were published previously in books and are reprinted here with permission: "A Bridge," *Six Vietnamese Poets*, Curbstone Press (2002); "Around the World," *Far Beyond Triage*, Calyx Books (2007); "At the Metolius River," *Red Jess*, Cherry Grove Collections (2006); "Blinking," *Moments Without Names: Selected Prose Poems*, White Pine (2002); "Blue Heron," *Millennial Spring*, Cloudbank Books (1999), also appeared in *Portland Lights*, Nine Lights Press (1999); "Bridgekeeper," *Portland Lights*, Nine Lights Press (1999); "Caroling," *Fortune*, Eastern Washington University Press (2007); "Celilo Fisherman," *These Few Words of Mine*, Blue Cloud Quarterly Press (1983); "Connections at Bear Wallow Creek," *Deer Drink the Moon*, Ooligan Press (2007); "Demographic," *Best American Poetry* (2006); "Detour," *Full Moon* (1980); "Dishwater," *Delights and Shadows*, Copper Canyon Press (2004); "Happiness," *New and Selected Poems, 1974–1994*, W. W. Norton & Co. (1989); "Heaven of the Moment," *Heaven of the Moment*, Bedbug Press (2007); "Lane Change," *A Bride of Narrow Escape*, Cloudbank Books (2006); "Martins Ferry," *Another Way to Begin*, Finishing Line Press (2006), also appeared in *As If Gravity Were a Theory*, Cider Press (2006); "Moon-Set," *In Our Own Voices*, Oregon Writers Colony (2006); "Notes on the St. Johns Bridge" (excerpt), *2 ½ Bridges*, 26 Books, (1999); "On the Stone Bridge at Multnomah Falls," *Poems for Twelve Moods*, Dragon's Teeth Press (1979); "Our Story," *The Way It Is*, Graywolf Press (1998); "Scaffolding," *Poems 1965–1975*, Farrar, Straus and Giroux (1980); "The Song of the Bridge," *I Built A Bridge And Other Poems*, The Davidson Press (1955); "The Whisperer," *Collected Poems*, Breitenbush Books (1979); "These Miles to My River, *The Hours of Us*, Finishing Line Press (2007); "Town is a Lamp in the Window," *Portland Lights*, Nine Lights Press (1999); "Traffic Jam on the Ross Island Bridge," *The Brink*, Gibbs Smith (2000); "Weather Poem," *Portland Lights*, Nine Lights Press (1999); "Where We Stand," *Voices from the Siskiyou* (2006), also appeared in *Deer Drink the Moon*, Ooligan Press (2007).

"Song For Us All," music by David York, was written for Stand Up Portland, an event that took place on the Portland waterfront in 1993.

Thank you to Kirsten Rian, poet, poem permissions and poet liaison, grant writer helper, and co-mother of and supporter of this book; to Kristin Thiel, a copy editor without peer who improved all the paragraphs we could give her

before she left on vacation; and to Amy Platt, for her deadline indexing. Thank you, too, to Joseph Boquiren for the cover art, and to Scott Bronson, a maker of maps from scratch. Others who helped: Judith Arcana followed an early draft for riding the Portland Aerial Tram, and Robert Fraser, a newcomer to Portland, carried my directions for the Three Bridge Central City Walk on a rainy Wednesday, afterward carefully explaining where I had lost him. Robert also provided the photo for the illustration on p. 44. More thanks to Doug Spangle, for guiding me through the recent history of the naming of the downtown grain elevators, and to Amtrak's Scott Hurd, Craig Kirkeby, and Tom Lynch, for the latest train yard history and timetables. Charlie White, always ready to explore, circled the city with me to make sure I'd gotten my on and off ramps straight. Bless especially Jennifer Omner, of ALL Publications, for stepping in as the book's designer when the original arrangements went south. Laura Foster's *Portland Hill Walks* (Timber Press, 2005) was an inspiration from the beginning. Thank you to all the bridge walkers, poets, musicians, street actors, and historians of all age who opened me to Portland's secrets, including the geologist Evelyn Pratt. Evelyn shook me to my itinerary the day she pointed out the ancient dirt holding up the east end of the Steel Bridge and the critters curled in the walls of Union Station. And thank you, the Outdoor Recreation branch of Portland Parks, and Multnomah County—Outdoor Rec for sanctioning the idea of taking people bridge walking in the first place, and the County for retrofitting room for us inside the Morrison Bridge. I also thank Lorin Schmit Dunlop, employed by the Regional Arts & Culture Council just long enough to be the bridge for the grant that partly funded this endeavor, and my sister Billie, for the rendering of the mother and her 15-month-old baby girl cantilevering a kiss. Of course, not a word of this would be complete without Ed Wortman, with this book a published illustrator of some of this city's greatest secrets. Every day Ed designs access to right thinking so even I—born left handed and half lost—can see it.
—SWW

Introduction: Bearings

As we finished the third edition of *The Portland Bridge Book*—225 pages of bridge opus, with 150 photographs, 25 drawings, two song lyrics, five poems, a 198-word glossary of structural terms, a transportation history timeline, a map, and comprehensive list of bridge owners and other resources—I realized we hadn't laid out even one walking route to help readers physically grip our subject.

Sitting in the shadows of the Marquam Bridge in July 2006, I called Lorin Schmit Dunlop at the Regional Arts & Culture Council. I'd seen RACC's call for project grants. I'd been gathering poems about bridges for a few years, my stockpile overflowing with poems by Northwest poets featured on my May-through-October Poetry & Bridge Walks for Portland Parks & Outdoor Recreation.

I asked Lorin what she thought of my chances for RACC funding a guidebook combining my favorite walking route with a dozen poems about bridges by mostly Northwest poets and a few of my own. I'd been thinking about an anthology of the Willamette and Columbia's big river metaphors since reading and admiring *Stone and Steel: Paintings & Writings Celebrating the Bridges of New York City*, edited by the New York artist Bascove. If you want the bridges of New York City painted in every shade of luscious, and famous poems about bridges, that is the book.

Lorin encouraged me to submit my application, turned in on time only because Kirsten Rian helped guide me through RACC's on-line application process. Kirsten, poet, musician, knowledgeable grant writer, and friend, offered—if we succeeded—to help arrange the poems in a chapbook-size guidebook. What we got as a result of our call for poems about bridges was more than we wanted to leave out. Many of these poems go beyond Portland, beyond Oregon, beyond continents.

As far as full-scale bridge walking directions, I promised RACC a set of self-guided directions for walking three Central City bridges (Morrison, Steel, Union Station Pedestrian Bridge). But once I started picking and choosing, I saw that the book would be underweight without at least four additional explorations, each different and for travel by vehicle, Amtrak, Portland Aerial Tram, and other public transportation. I soon realized the guide part of this book was an opportunity to finally set down for posterity my most traveled bridge walking and driving directions. What it's not meant to do is replace the third edition of *The Portland Bridge Book*, published in November 2006. Those who want to know more about a bridge might keep the third edition close—I direct the reader to many of its pages for further reference.

In addition to the "Three Bridge Central City Walk (with Options)," a route I've honed leading walks for Parks since 1991, I've also included "Amtrak from Portland, Oregon, All the Way to Vancouver, Washington Over Three Movable Bridges—and Back." Based on a class I created for Saturday Academy in 2002, I show the ins and outs of boarding Amtrak at Portland's Union Station to ride across two 1908 swing spans and a converted vertical lift and then what to sketch, photograph, or look for when arriving at Vancouver Station Depot.

And once I figured out it was free to ride downhill, I had to give public directions to the 3,300-foot-long Portland Aerial Tram, the first steel rope strand structure in Oregon designed to carry people across four major highways in two minutes and fifty seconds. Between January and October 2007, I've led more than 800 students and adults up to (and down from) Pill Hill, so you can trust my well-practiced directions in "A Free Ride on the Bridge that's the Portland Aerial Tram."

The two remaining explorations are the "Circle of Portland Counting 52 Bridges in Less Than Eight Minutes Without Breaking the Speed Limit," and "From the (Repaired) Crack in the Fremont Bridge to the Burlington Northern Santa Fe Railway Bridge 5.1 to the St. Johns Bridge to the Sauvie Island Bridge to the Hanging Deck Truss Carrying NW Thurman St. Over Balch Gulch."

The "Circle of Portland Counting 52 Bridges" is an exercise that I've incorporated into an annual Portland Bridges class I've taught at OMSI for the past 15 years. This drive-around is best done with one or more passengers counting bridges near and far while the driver keeps her eyes on the road.

"From the (Repaired) Crack in the Fremont Bridge" is a five-bridge itinerary that takes you to the longest, most modified, most elegant, newest, and oldest of Portland's highway and railroad bridges. My research for this 25-miler dates to November 1993, the year *The Oregonian* paid me $100 to write about the raising of the Fremont Bridge's center span 20 years before. As part of my research, I interviewed Ed Wortman. Ed had worked as the field engineer directing the ironworkers (as much as anyone directs an ironworker) in Fremont's construction. One interview with Ed led to others. After the story was published, the Maine native called and invited me to dinner at Ken's Home Plate on SE Hawthorne Blvd. For dessert, he took me to the two 16-foot-tall bearings, also called shoes, holding up the west end of the Fremont Bridge.

We parked in the lot at 1750 NW Naito Pkwy., stepping up onto a concrete pad on the west bank of the Willamette River. Ed held my hands against the southwest shoe and where a constant 7,500 tons of gravity manacles the ground. Doing the math: four shoes times 7,500 tons meant Fremont weighs 30,000 tons! Be still the Newton part of my heart.

Ed also pointed to the crack in one of the tie girders that almost brought down Fremont's west side span across Front Avenue in 1971, only 250 feet from where we stood on the bearing pad. Talk about opening my eyes to secrets in the built environment. What *Walking Bridges* aims to do is follow Ed's example, to tell the secret of a bridge and its appurtenances that might not otherwise be known. Many of the surprises I've discovered in my 23-year bridge career are included in all five explorations.

Due to the RACC requirement that we print before December 31, 2007, we were faced with a brief period to advertise for and accept submissions. It looks now as if we've only scratched the surface of what's possible to read into a bridge, whether a bridge from here or far away.

Last, I see this book as a process, like Bessemer's, where pig iron—in this case a raw idea—is purified in an open hearth until what you hold in your hand is smooth, load-bearing steel. I see a second edition where more poems about bridges (real and metaphorical) will hold additional and important sway. Meanwhile, I hope you will be amazed by the places a bridge can carry a mind despite stanzas confined to paper and its strict margins.

Sharon Wood Wortman
November 2007

Walking Bridges Using Poetry as a Compass

PORTLAND & VICINITY

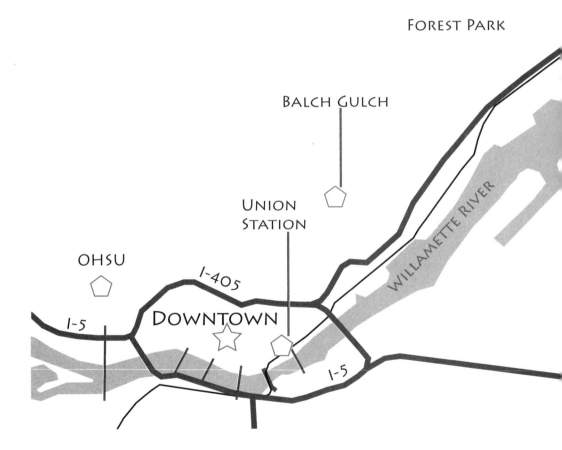

FOREST PARK

BALCH GULCH

WILLAMETTE RIVER

UNION
STATION

OHSU

I-405

I-5

DOWNTOWN

I-5

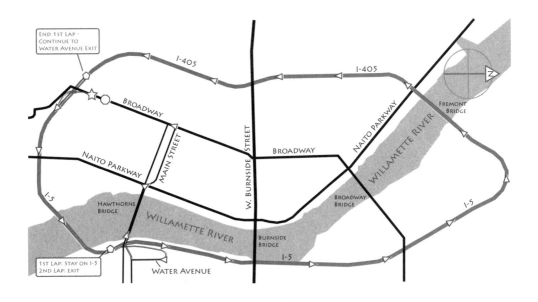

END 1ST LAP -
CONTINUE TO
WATER AVENUE EXIT

I-405

I-405

BROADWAY

NAITO PARKWAY

WILLAMETTE RIVER

FREMONT
BRIDGE

MAIN STREET

NAITO PARKWAY

W. BURNSIDE STREET

BROADWAY

I-5

HAWTHORNE
BRIDGE

WILLAMETTE RIVER

BROADWAY
BRIDGE

I-5

I-5

BURNSIDE
BRIDGE

1ST LAP: STAY ON I-5
2ND LAP: EXIT

WATER AVENUE

I-5

☆ START
— ROUTE
▦ RAILROAD
▷ DIRECTION
○ FINISH

Exploration One

This drive-around begins and ends near SW Sixth Ave.

➤ Count 52 highway bridges in a loop of the Marquam (Interstate 5) and Fremont (Interstate 405) bridges. You'll need at least two people: someone behind the steering wheel who keeps his or her eyes on the road at all times, and at least one passenger to do the counting (a school bus loaded with students is even better). Fifty-two—count them—is the number of highway bridges, including approaches, that a vehicle's tires touch, cross over, or cross under while completing this round-trip. The stretch to the west of downtown along I-405 is particularly instructive, with bridges overhead faster than you can say "200-foot-long blocks."

Basics

Distance: 6.5 miles. You can begin from any entrance point around the loop as long as you exit the loop where you began or stop counting when you pass your entry point.

Time: Eight minutes (during non-rush hours and without exceeding the posted speed limit). Traffic around the loop is thinner between 10 a.m. and 1:30 p.m.

Bridges Counted: 52
Equipment needed: Stop watch and a working odometer

Site Specifics

The definition of a bridge, according to the Federal Highway Administration, is any span or structure across an opening 20 feet or greater. In the United States that means 600,000 highway bridges. Oregon has about 6,700 highway bridges, with some of the largest, oldest, rarest, and most earthquake-vulnerable on the Willamette River in Portland. This number includes approach and exit ramps, each one given its own designation number and safety inspections.

The freeway loop between the Marquam Bridge, on the south, and Fremont Bridge, on the north, was completed with the opening of the Fremont Bridge in 1973. I-405, also known as the Stadium Freeway, connects downtown Portland west of the Willamette River to I-5, completed in Portland in 1966.

Prior to 1973, vehicles moved along the west side of the Willamette River via Harbor Drive. With the opening of the Eastbank Freeway, Harbor Drive was no longer needed. Governor Tom McCall created a task force in 1968 to study proposals for creating a public open space in its place. In 1974, Harbor Drive was torn up and construction of a waterfront park began. It was dedicated in 1978 and renamed Governor Tom McCall Waterfront Park in 1984.

Many would like to see I-5 taken off the Eastbank, a costly proposal. Until that happens, Marquam affords one of the finest north-south views, best appreciated in the inevitable slow traffic you'll encounter morning and afternoon, Monday through Friday.

Putting It Into Gear

1. Begin at the entrance to I-5 located in the University District in SW Portland, entering I-5 from SW Broadway, immediately south of SW Jackson St.

2. Follow the signs "The Dalles-Salem," passing under the first three bridges. Stay right.

3. Follow the signs "North I-5—East 84 The Dalles-Seattle," crossing under SW Naito Pkwy. and onto the top deck of the Marquam Bridge.

4. Traffic merges on top of the bridge; move to the left lanes.

5. Follow the signs "I-5 North/Seattle." That's the Oregon Convention Center in the distance, with its identical twin towers.

6. In the stretch where I-5 sits on the ground, you pass under (and count) ten more bridges. Stay left, past the Rose Quarter arena (on your left).

7. Follow the signs "I-405—30 West St. Helens ¾ mile."

8. Move to the right lane, passing under bridges carrying Weidler St., Broadway, Vancouver Ave., and Flint Ave.

9. Follow signs "St. Helens-West."

10. Take exit 302B.

11. Drive over the top of the Fremont Bridge, moving to the left-hand lanes. If there isn't too much traffic, you may be able to see the small ladder that drops from under the north arch rib, just above the bridge's highway deck. This is the entrance for the maintenance workers to climb inside the arch to the flagpole elevation and once, in 1993, a writer curious about bridges.

12. You pass over five more bridges going down to ground level.

13. Follow the signs "I-405 City Center-Beaverton West 26." You'll see the Pearl District on your left. Stay left, passing under a bridge at the end of nearly every block, to name a few: NW Everett St., NW Couch St., West Burnside, SW 14th Ave., SW Morrison St., SW Taylor St., and SW Salmon St.

14. Follow signs "26 East-Sixth Ave.-Ross Island Bridge-½ mile."

15. Move to the right lane, following The Dalles-Seattle exit, 1C.

16. Stop counting bridges at the Sixth Ave. overpass.

17. Once across the Marquam Bridge, take the first exit to the right, for I-84, and then take the first exit marked "OMSI-Central Eastside Industrial District."

18. Turn right onto SE Water Ave., where Water intersects with SE Yamhill St.

19. Travel five blocks south on Water, passing the Multnomah County Bridge Engineering and Maintenance offices at 1403 SE Water Ave. (on the right, under the east end approaches of the Hawthorne Bridge).

20. Just past the County offices, turn right onto SE Hawthorne Boulevard, and cross the Hawthorne Bridge back to the west side, or keep traveling south or east, on the side of the river where day first balances the sunrise.

Portland

City of the short blocks
stretching our legs

Rainburg
Double-sided river urge:

Throat through which ocean bearing
ships cough grain

City with its head cranked west
Rest of the body sprawled east:

Gut flattened for the sake of trains
For the sake of the masses

City always pushing the boundaries
and growing like trees:

City with a wide girth thinned by parks
. . . and dropped in the middle

A freeway-shaped heart
Fed by bridges carrying blood

In fifty-two directions at once
This city with rosy cheeks—SWW

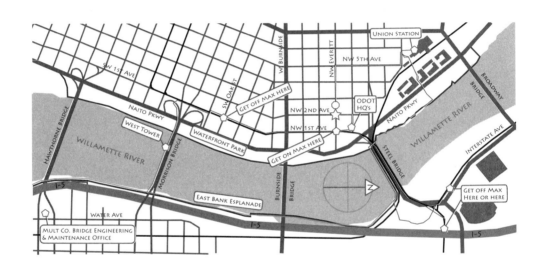

WILLAMETTE RIVER

SW 1st Ave

Naito Pkwy

West Tower

Waterfront Park

SW Oak St

Get off Max here

Hawthorne Bridge

Morrison Bridge

East Bank Esplanade

I-5

Water Ave

Mult Co. Bridge Engineering
& Maintenance Office

Burnside Bridge

W Burnside

NW Everett

NW 5th Ave

Union Station

NW 2nd Ave

ODOT HQ's

NW 1st Ave

Get on Max Here

I-5

Naito Pkwy

Steel Bridge

WILLAMETTE RIVER

Broadway Bridge

Interstate Ave

Get off Max
Here or here

I-5

N

☆ START
— ROUTE
▥ RAILROAD
▷ DIRECTION
○ FINISH

Exploration Two

THREE BRIDGE CENTRAL CITY WALK
(WITH OPTIONS)

This trip begins and ends in Old Town.

➤ See a plaque marking Portland's 1894 flood.

➤ Visit a bridge museum (open Monday-Friday, 7:00 a.m.–5 p.m.).

➤ Walk to the center span of a bascule bridge where you can stand with one foot in SE Portland and one in SW Portland.

➤ Ride Metropolitan Area Express (MAX) light rail across the Willamette River.

➤ Walk on a $2.5 million sidewalk cantilevered off the railroad deck of a unique double-deck truss bridge.

➤ See some of the oldest exposed dirt original to Portland.

➤ Walk along the Willamette Greenway Trail in the working part of Portland Harbor.

➤ Jump on a flexible footbridge in a test for synchronous vertical excitation.

➤ Count fossils from the time of the dinosaurs, embedded in the limestone walls of Portland Union Train Station.

➤ Options: Walking on the Eastbank Esplanade, the Burnside Bridge, the Hawthorne Bridge, the Eastbank Esplanade Floating Bridge; walking by Broadway Bridge's Pier IV (with record-setting foundations); and walking across the Frank Ivancie Footbridge.

Basics

Distance: Without options, one to two miles. It is one-third mile between Hawthorne, Morrison, Burnside, Steel, and Broadway bridges.

Time: one to two hours

ADA: The circle ramp of Morrison Bridge's east end, leading to the mile-long Vera Katz Eastbank Esplanade, is too steep for most wheelchair users. The lift from the Esplanade to the Burnside Bridge's southeast sidewalk is scheduled to be replaced with an elevator. Otherwise, the Esplanade–Governor Tom McCall Waterfront Park loop—two miles round-trip—is accessible.

TriMet buses serving NW Second Ave. and NW Everett St: #4, #8, #10, #33, #35, #44, and #77; one block east, at NW First Ave. and Everett is the Old Town/Chinatown MAX Station. To the west three-four blocks is the Portland Transit Mall, under construction to carry MAX trains beginning in 2009. Meanwhile, buses pick up and deliver on NW Third Ave. (northbound) and NW Fourth Ave. (southbound).

Fareless Square: Riders do not pay to ride MAX, TriMet buses, and the Portland Streetcar in the Central City. Fareless Square on MAX extends to the east side and the Lloyd District. MAX consists of three lines, all three running through downtown: Blue line from Gresham to Hillsboro, Red line from Portland International Airport to Beaverton, and Yellow line from the Exposition Center to Downtown.

For more about Fareless Square, go to <www.trimet.org/fares/fareless> or call 503 238-RIDE.

Site Specifics

Portland's most prominent physical feature is the Willamette River, the reason for 12 bridges from Sellwood to Sauvie Island. Because the river was here first, all water-borne vessels have the right of way. Thus, bridges must be built high enough or move out of the way to allow clear passage.

Due to changes along the waterfront south of the Steel Bridge (the big bridge with black towers and counterweights that move up and down), it is difficult to know why Portland was settled a dozen miles up the Willamette River. This is because the Willamette was the Interstate 5 of the 1800s—the only way then to move manufactured goods and crops into and out of Portland during European settlement. Portland is still one of a handful of inland river port cities in the United States that can handle deep draft ships. On the east bank north of the Steel Bridge, giant ocean-going vessels take on grain at two large elevators almost every day.

The grain elevator closest to downtown used to be called LDC (for Louis-Dreyfus Co.), and before that Globe, but it's now CLD "O" Dock. The elevator just south of the Broadway Bridge was Bunge, then Irving, and is now CLD Irving. You can see the cranes of the Port of Portland, downriver (north) of the Fremont Bridge. Also watch for sea lions, cormorants, peregrines, bald eagles, red tailed hawks, the great blue heron (Portland's official city bird), ducks, and Canada geese, well fed by grain spillage. Farther down the river, at Kelley Point Park (Willamette River mile zero), the Willamette meets the Columbia River.

Two steel vertical lift bridges (Hawthorne and Steel) and two bascule bridges (Morrison and Burnside) link Waterfront Park and the Eastbank Esplanade, like an adjustable zipper. The beauty and genius of this corner of the Willamette, a 45-degree curve near the Steel Bridge, is that you can begin your loop on either side of the river, getting on and off the bridges at convenient points. On the east side, all four bridges connect to the Eastbank Esplanade. On the west side, the Hawthorne and Steel bridges connect to the park, while the west ends of the Burnside and Morrison bridges are accessible one block west of the park, along First.

Vertical lift and bascule bridges use weights to counterbalance and lift their roadway decks. A vertical lift bridge's roadway deck lifts up and down much like an elevator—the concrete counterweights in the towers balance the weight of the deck as it moves. The twin Interstate (I-5) Bridges, across the Columbia River between Portland and Vancouver, Washington also are vertical lift bridges. Bascule bridges open more like a double-door cupboard, but one that tilts skyward. Bascule is a French word for seesaw. Bascule bridges have weights on both sides of a beam and when the heavier weight (usually made of concrete) goes down on one side of the pivot point, the lighter weight (roadway deck) moves up on the other side. The Broadway Bridge, the big red bridge just north of the Steel Bridge, is another bascule, but the Broadway's counterweights are above the river piers, while the Morrison and Burnside's counterweights are inside the river piers. Another difference is that the Broadway rolls backwards as it opens. The third common type of movable bridges is the swing bridge. See p. 59 for more about swing bridges. For drawings of these movable bridges and how they work, see pp. 143–154 in the third edition of *The Portland Bridge Book*.

More about the Willamette River

The Willamette, like the Nile, Monongahela, Yellowstone, and several other rivers, flows north. By the time the Willamette arrives in Portland Harbor, it's carrying the Willamette Valley's entire drainage. Tributaries include the Long Tom, Santiam, Luckiamute, Yamhill, Molalla, Tualatin, and Clackamas rivers, plus many creeks, including Johnson Creek. There are no dams on the main stem, but 13 on its tributaries. The Willamette often backs up at the end of its journey, looking like a bathtub with a clogged drain, especially if ocean tides are pushing inland. Most noticeable when the river is low, the Pacific—115 river miles west of downtown Portland—shoves twice a day against the Columbia River, only 12.8 miles north (downriver) of the Morrison Bridge. The Columbia then shoves against the Willamette as far south (upriver) as the falls at Oregon City, located at Willamette River mile 26.

To walk the Willamette's features from headwaters to Kelley Point Park, go to the Esplanade between the northeast end of the Hawthorne Bridge and Portland Fire Station #7. The river is cast in bronze in the plaza, and you can walk its length in two minutes. Also along the waterfront, you can find kayaks to rent, and the cruise ship *Spirit of Portland*. Willamette River Jet Boats, docked at the Oregon Museum of Science and Industry (OMSI), also knows its bridges.

To receive a calendar with free family events, go to the Web site of River Renaissance, a citywide partnership to revitalize the Willamette in Portland, <www.portlandonline.com/river>, or call 503-823-0275. Also see Exploration Four "From the (Repaired) Crack in the Fremont Bridge, to the Burlington Northern Santa Fe Railway Bridge 5.1 to the St. Johns Bridge to the Sauvie Island Bridge to the Hanging Deck Truss Carrying NW Thurman St. Over Balch Gulch."

Waterfront Bridge Events

In addition to the annual fundraising walks/runs and the Portland Marathon, two other annual events involve the downtown bridges:

• Bridge Pedal, sponsored by Providence Hospital and others, is held the second Sunday of every August (August 10 in 2008). In 2007, 20,000 people walked or biked the Central City bridges in this annual morning event. Web site: <www.providence.org/oregon/events/bridge_pedal>.

• Portland Parks and Outdoor Recreation sponsors Poetry & Bridges walks May through October. Each walk, about a mile long, features a Portland-area poet, and, weather willing, a visit to the operator's tower and bascule pit of the Morrison Bridge. Call PP&R at 503-823-5132, or visit <www.bridgestories.com>.

Orientation: Block Zero and Other Getting-Around Hints

▶ Although this itinerary does not begin at the Burnside Bridge, a movable designed in the Italian Renaissance style of architecture and Portland's only bridge with two red roofs, it helps to know that the Burnside Bridge and the Willamette River form Block Zero in the city's street grid. Everything east of the Willamette is east Portland, west of the Willamette is west Portland, north of the Burnside Bridge is north Portland, and south of the Burnside Bridge is south Portland. Thus, you are either in NE, NW, SE, or SW Portland, depending on your proximity to the Burnside Bridge and the Willamette River. For example, if you live near SE 122nd Ave. and SE Foster Rd., you're south of the Burnside Bridge, east of the Willamette River and because the street numbering system (each side of the river) begins at the river, you live 122 blocks from the Willamette. North Portland, hemmed in by the Willamette and Columbia rivers, is called the Peninsula and is the city's fifth section. The St. Johns Bridge, on the Peninsula at Willamette River mile 5.8, is upriver (south) from Willamette River mile 0.

▶ The streets in NW Portland, and only in NW Portland, are alphabetized, i.e., Burnside, Couch, Davis, Everett, Flanders, Glisan, Hoyt streets, etc. Naito Pkwy., mentioned many times in this book, was Front Ave. until 1996, when it was renamed in honor of William Naito (1926–1996), for his many civic contributions. Bill Naito (pronounced nate-oh and nite-oh) was also the mover for the creation of the Japanese American Historical Plaza, which honors Japanese-American heritage. The plaza, between the Steel and Burnside bridges in Waterfront Park, is the only memorial in the U.S. dedicated to the Bill of Rights.

➤ SW and NW Broadway are actually SW and NW Seventh Ave.

➤ Portland's blocks are 200 feet on each side. Motorists here are famous for pulling up to intersections, looking left, and turning right. For more about Portland walking and bicycling, go to the Web sites of the Willamette Pedestrian Coalition <www.americawalks.org/wpc/>, and the Bicycle Transportation Alliance: <www.bita4bikes.org/>.

➤ About panhandling: One citizen, new to Portland, hands out gift certificates to fast food restaurants in downtown Portland. Another asks the person asking for money if he or she is hungry. The answer 90 percent of the time is yes—her cue, she says, to walk with the person to the nearest street cart, deli, fast food counter, convenience store, or sit-down restaurant—food being easier to find in Portland than bridge ramps. She invites the person to order what they want and then she pays and excuses herself. Time, she notices, is the commodity the privileged are most deficient in and find difficult to give away. For more about the meal coupons and programs of the Sisters of the Road Café, go to <www.sistersoftheroad.org>.

High-Water Mark

1. Begin on the steps on the corner of NW Second and Everett, three blocks north of Burnside. This is the 13-story Northwest Natural Building, also called One Pacific Square, in Portland's Skidmore/Old Town Historic District.

Look for the high-water marker on the twentieth century brick retaining wall in the middle of the block between Everett and Davis. The marker, about four feet above the sidewalk, is next to a set of brick steps. It shows the height of the Willamette's penetration into the Central City at 11 a.m., June 7, 1894. Another high water year was 1964 and then, in 1996, the river threatened to overtake the bottom deck of the Steel Bridge and the Portland Harbor Wall. It did succeed in flooding the first floor units at McCormick Pier Apartments, located farther downriver (north).

HIGH WATER MARKER IN OLD TOWN

Bridge Museum

2. Cross Everett at Second and walk one block north to 123 NW Flanders St., and the Oregon Dept. of Transportation Region 1 headquarters, open 7:00 a.m.–5:00 p.m. weekdays. The concrete wall just north of Region 1 is the Glisan St. ramp off the Steel Bridge. The tiled-roof building across the street from ODOT is the teahouse in the Portland Classical Chinese Garden. The tall building above the garden is the U.S. Bancorp Building, nicknamed Big Pink (see p. 60 for more about Big Pink). To the north, through the NW Natural parking lot, across the street from ODOT, you can see parts of the Union Station Pedestrian Bridge, the Fremont Bridge, and the Broadway Bridge.

Ask the security person at ODOT's front desk (everyone who enters the building must sign in) for permission to visit the Historic American Engineering Record (HAER)-National Parks Service Willamette River Bridges exhibit. It is located on the first floor, at the rear of the building, past the bathrooms. You can operate an old (1926) control panel from the Burnside Bridge, pick up a hefty piece of steel cable, and study a photograph of the first Steel Bridge, a double-deck swing span. There is also a 40-year-old model of the Fremont Bridge. *Quiet* is the word here—about 350 ODOT employees work at Region 1, which is also the site of the Traffic Management Operation Center. The TMOC dispatchers monitor about 120 cameras 24 hours a day, 365 days a year. Their job is to keep traffic moving. More than a million vehicles cross the Willamette and Columbia river bridges in the metro area every day. In 1947, when I was three years old, there were about 400,000 registered vehicles in Oregon; now there are more than four million. For more about road conditions, go to <www.tripcheck.com> or call 511. For more about the HAER histories, photographs, and drawings, see pp. 135–148 in the third edition of *The Portland Bridge Book*.

Metropolitan Area Express (MAX) Light Rail

3. Backtrack from ODOT to First and Everett; board MAX at the Old Town/Chinatown Station westbound on any train (Blue, Red, or Yellow). At this point, westbound means going south, toward downtown and away from the Willamette River and the Steel Bridge. MAX, operated by TriMet, opened across the Steel Bridge in 1986. TriMet is a municipal corporation providing public transportation for much of the three counties in the metro area. About 1,300 drivers operate in a 44-mile, 64-station MAX light rail system, plus 92 bus lines.

4. Ride MAX two stops south, passing under the west end of the Burnside Bridge and past Skidmore Fountain, to the Oak St./SW First Ave. station.

5. Walk to the end of the block to First and SW Stark St., then cross either First or Stark, but get to the intersection's southeast corner and on the same side of the street as the Morrison Bridge's north end cloverleaf ramp.

6. Staying on the sidewalk, follow the MAX tracks one block south. Pass TriMet's small brick building (sign reads "High Voltage") on the left and approach the second set of concrete steps. This second set of steps leads under the Morrison Bridge's southwest cloverleaf ramp.

Morrison Bridge

7. Walk between the chain-link fences under the ramp. Looking up, you'll see some of the ramp's plate girders, cross braces, webs, and rivets.

> About the Morrison Bridge: There have been three Morrison Bridges, the first opened in 1887 and was the first to span the lower Willamette River. The second bridge, also a swing span, opened in 1905. The bridge

today dates to 1958, the same year the hula-hoop was invented. It's a tossup whether the operator towers, minimalist in design, look more like airport control towers or penitentiary towers. One nice touch is the curved shape the engineers gave to the bridge's bottom chords, better seen from Waterfront Park. The Morrison turns 50 in 2008, becoming eligible for the National Register of Historic Places. Each leaf in its bascule span is balanced by a 950-ton counterweight, or as one Brooklyn third grader figured during a bridge walk, the same weight as 11 adult male brachiosaurus dinosaurs. Two 36-foot-tall gears and two 100-horsepower motors move each counterweight, and during a lift the bridge does make a prehistoric-sounding groan. For more about the Morrison Bridge, see pp. 53–60 in the third edition of *The Portland Bridge Book*. To see a virtual lift, go to <www.bridgestories.com>.

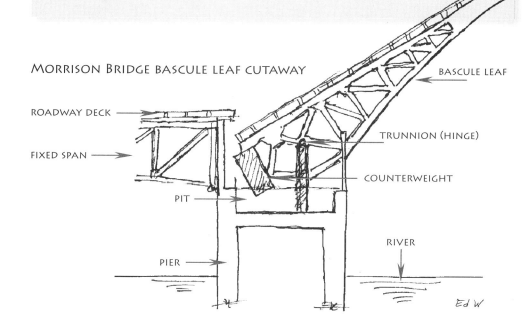

MORRISON BRIDGE BASCULE LEAF CUTAWAY

BASCULE LEAF

ROADWAY DECK

TRUNNION (HINGE)

FIXED SPAN

COUNTERWEIGHT

PIT

RIVER

PIER

Ed W

8. In a dozen steps, just past the chain-link, you'll be standing at the edge of a large surface parking lot.

9. Make a hard left (north) and walk up a concrete stairway (23 steps) to the bridge's southwest sidewalk. There is also an ADA ramp located at Naito and SW Morrison St., half a block farther south. Multnomah County plans to make the sidewalks on the Morrison Bridge better for pedestrians and bicyclists in the near future.

Things to See from the Morrison Bridge

10. Continue across the Morrison Bridge to the first (west end) operator's tower and covered viewing area. You can see plenty from this vantage point:

The arch-shaped wooden structures pointing upriver (south) at water level are starlings, also called dolphins. One at each bascule pier, they protect from ships or debris smashing into the piers.

MORRISON BRIDGE
OPERATOR'S TOWER
AND STARLING

Looking toward the Portland Harbor Wall on the west side of the river, you can see the ghost of the 1905 Morrison. Its outline, moss-free and a different color than the rest of the wall, is between markers 32 and 33, about 250 feet south of the bridge's west approach ramp. This second Morrison Bridge stood until today's bridge opened. This is why the Morrison Bridge doesn't connect with Morrison St. on the west side. There is a picture in one of the interpretive panels on the East-bank Esplanade showing bridge number two still in use while number three was under construction. Those black tire-studded bumpers anchored against the mile-long Harbor Wall keep ships from scraping against concrete.

THE GHOST OF THE 1905 MORRISON BRIDGE ON THE HARBOR WALL, WITH A BUMPER IN THE FOREGROUND

GHOST

HARBOR WALL

Ed W

Find the white spots in the railing across the traffic lanes on the north side of the bridge, just below the directional sign. The spots indicate where repairs were made in the railing in 2005, after a driver spun out of control on the grating of the Morrison Bridge and drove off the bridge to the bottom of the Willamette River. She escaped with only minor scrapes and bruises.

This overlook is the perfect place to count bridges. On the north side of the Morrison Bridge, look for the Fremont (way off to the left), the Broadway (red top chords seen to the left of the green glass of the Northwest Natural Building), the Steel, the Burnside, and the East-bank Esplanade Floating Bridge. On the south side of the Morrison Bridge, you can see the Hawthorne, the double-deck Marquam, the Ross Island, the 660-foot-long Veterans Hospital Skybridge, and the Portland Aerial Tram—the latter two high in the West Hills. And don't forget to count approach ramps, or any other crossing 20 feet or longer. The definition of a bridge, according to the Federal Highway Administration, is any span across an opening 20 feet or greater.

That historic steam tug anchored at the foot of SW Pine St., on the Harbor Wall between the Burnside and Morrison bridges, is the Oregon Maritime Museum. As a member, you can see the Christmas Ship Parade and Fourth of July fireworks from a front seat on the river. For more about the sternwheeler *Portland*, go to <www.oregonmaritimemuseum.org>.

The last thing to look for is the curve in the Willamette River just before the Steel Bridge. If you've thought of the river as running straight through the Central City, you can see it does not. There is a second curve, to the south, at the Ross Island Bridge.

In the Middle of Morrison a Foot in Each Side of Portland

11. Leave the covered viewing area and walk across the Morrison Bridge (heading east) to the center of the bascule span where the west leaf and east leaf meet in the middle of the Willamette River. This is an exercise for days when it isn't raining—the grating on the Morrison Bridge's bascule span deck is worn out after 50 years of use and can be slippery for vehicles exceeding the speed limit or changing lanes. It is illegal to change lanes on the grating when driving across the Morrison Bridge.

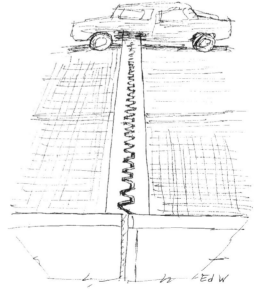

Straddle the gap in the sidewalk where the leaves come together at center span and you'll be standing with one foot in SE Portland and one foot in SW Portland. SE Portland is part of what once was East Portland, a separate city incorporated into Portland in 1891, the same year W.L. Hudson invented the zipper.

Options: Eastbank Esplanade, Steel Bridge, and Burnside Bridge

From center span, you can continue across the Willamette, exiting from the Morrison Bridge down the circle ramp to the Eastbank Esplanade. Staying on the southeast sidewalk, you can also exit the Morrison Bridge one block farther east, at SE Water Ave.

Once on the Eastbank Esplanade (facing the river), you can turn right (north) toward the Steel and Burnside bridges, or turn left (south), toward the Hawthorne Bridge.

About the Eastbank Esplanade: A little over a mile in length, the $31 million Esplanade opened in 2001. It is a pedestrian and bicycle trail funded by the Oregon Dept. of Transportation and the City of Portland that makes it possible for users to walk the length of the east bank in the Central City. Before the Esplanade, users could only go as far as the circle ramp on the east end of the Morrison Bridge, as access to the east ends of the Burnside and Steel bridges was cut off by I-5. Contributing to the Esplanade's high cost is the 1,200-foot-long aluminum bridge and floating concrete walkway at the Esplanade's north end that solved the problem of getting around I-5. Fourteen urban markers stand at intersections along the Esplanade, noting where city streets historically met the riverfront. In addition, there are 19 porcelain enamel and steel interpretive panels with story themes chronicling the history and evolution of the riverfront. The themes for the panels include transportation, commerce, east side and west side development, bridges, and ecology of the river. Mayer/Reed, a landscape architecture and environmental graphics firm, designed the Esplanade with KPFF Consulting Engineers, both of Portland.

EASTBANK ESPLANADE
ANKENY ST. URBAN MARKER

BURNSIDE BRIDGE OPERATOR'S TOWER

About the Burnside Bridge: The counterweights inside Burnside's bascule piers, nearly 2,000 tons each, weigh double Morrison's counterweights. Burnside was the first major bascule bridge in the U.S. with a concrete deck, so the counterweights required to lift the deck had to be designed large. Opened in 1926, it is now the city's Lifeline Corridor. In case of catastrophe, Burnside has been designated to carry emergency equipment and vehicles. Under Burnside's east end piers is a very large and much used public skateboard ramp, featured in the movie *Free Willy*. Notice, if you go here, that the big steel girders above the ramp are encased in concrete, probably for fire protection. The concrete makes the girders extra heavy and even more vulnerable to earthquake. I tell people who take my bridge walks to enjoy Portland while it's here.

About the Steel Bridge (see p. 59).

Urban myth: There are not too many of these in Portland, unless you count the Shanghai tunnels, or the claim that the St. Johns Bridge (downriver at Willamette River mile 5.6) was the model for the Golden Gate Bridge. The only direct connection a major Portland bridge has with the Golden Gate and its champion Joseph Strauss is that the opening mechanism on the Burnside was designed and patented by Strauss. For more about the Burnside Bridge, see pp. 45–52 in the third edition of *The Portland Bridge Book*. For more about the "so-called tunnels," see "Portland's buried truth," by Helen Jung, *The Oregonian*, October 4, 2007.

Things to See Along the Optional Path
(Eastbank Esplanade to the Hawthorne Bridge)

About the Hawthorne Bridge: Opened in 1910, this is the oldest operating vertical lift bridge in the U.S., and it may be the oldest anywhere in the world. As poet Diane Holland has written: "It's honest, sturdy, yet eloquent architecture. I love that it is what it is." The faded sidewalk railing (painted red in 1999) was designed at a height to keep horses from jumping over the side. The Hawthorne Bridge is now Bridge Central, with the operator here taking calls to coordinate openings on the Morrison and Burnside bridges, which do not have full-time operators. Because of its age, Hawthorne is opened at least once every eight hours ship or no. For more about the Hawthorne Bridge, see pp. 61–68 in the third edition of *The Portland Bridge Book.*

RAILING OF 1910 HAWTHORNE BRIDGE,
DESIGNED TO KEEP HORSES FROM JUMPING OVER THE SIDE

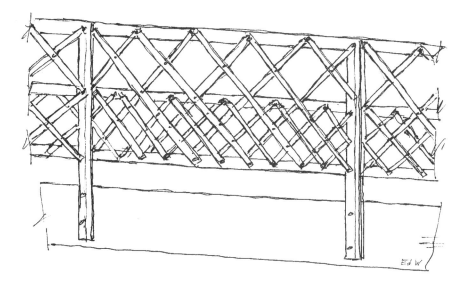

There is a river height gauge at the south end of the Harbor Wall, just southwest of the Hawthorne Bridge. The gauge reads from zero to 24 feet. The Hawthorne Bridge operator refers to it for navigational purposes on the Willamette. When tugboat operators, for example, want to know how much clearance they have, the Hawthorne Bridge operator looks out and reads the gauge. Each bridge must be adjusted to what the gauge shows. The Hawthorne Bridge has 49 feet of clearance when the gauge is showing zero. If the gauge reads two feet, then this means 47 feet of clearance. With two feet showing on the gauge, a captain of a 40-foot-tall sailboat knows she has seven feet of clearance. Other clearances at zero water: Broadway Bridge 90 feet, Steel Bridge (highway deck) 72 feet, Steel Bridge (railroad deck) 26 feet, Burnside Bridge 64 feet, Morrison Bridge 69 feet.

RIVER GAUGE AT THE SOUTH END OF THE PORTLAND HARBOR WALL

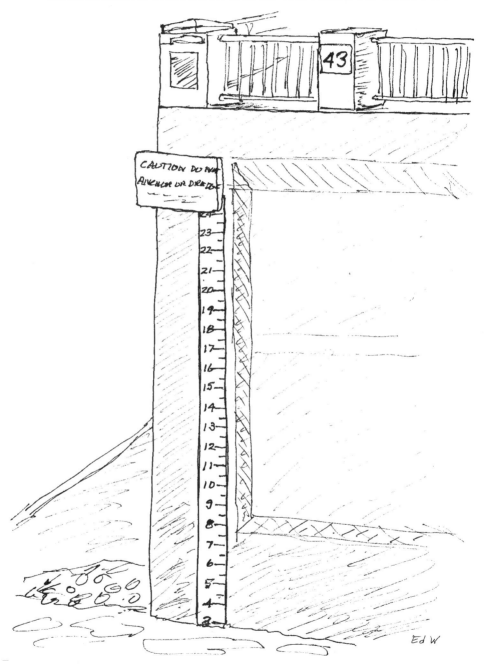

Just to the north of the Hawthorne Bridge is a bronze map of the Willamette River, inset in the plaza of the Eastbank Esplanade (see p. 41). OMSI sits three blocks south of Hawthorne, and the Willamette Jet Boats dock is just south of the Marquam Bridge. The sidewalk along here is the Greenway Trail on the east side of the Willamette and connects with the Springwater Corridor, a paved 21-mile pedestrian and bicycle path winding from the Ross Island Bridge past Oaks Amusement Park, through Gresham, to Boring, Oregon. The Esplanade, Waterfront Park, and Springwater Corridor are all part of the 140-Mile-Loop, a system of hiking and walking trails in the metro area.

Multnomah County's Bridge Engineering and Maintenance office, 1403 SE Water Ave., is located under the east end approach ramps of the Hawthorne Bridge. Multnomah County owns and operates the Hawthorne, Morrison, Burnside, and Broadway bridges; the Sellwood Bridge, father upstream; and the Sauvie Island Bridge, on the Multnomah Channel of the Willamette River, four miles from the St. Johns Bridge.

If you walk across the Hawthorne Bridge (on the south or north sidewalk), you return to Waterfront Park, and just to the north is Salmon Street Springs. Notice under the west end of the Hawthorne Bridge how one of the bridge's river piers is buried in the asphalt adjacent to the Harbor Wall. When the Hawthorne Bridge opened in 1910, this pier was in the Willamette River. Before the Harbor Wall was finished in 1929, the river extended to Front (now Naito).

HAWTHORNE BRIDGE RIVER PIER BURIED IN TOM MCCALL WATERFRONT PARK

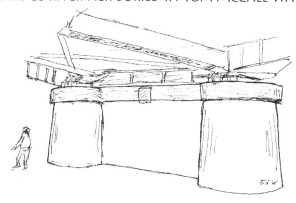

Continuing the Basic Itinerary:
MAX over the Steel Bridge and across the Willamette River

12. From the middle of the Morrison Bridge, retrace your steps, backtracking from Morrison's west end stairs and under the west end approach ramps to the Oak St./SW First St. MAX station.

MAX across the Willamette River
Eastbank Esplanade Railroad Overcrossing Bridge

13. Board any color MAX train headed away from downtown and ride west to east across the Steel Bridge.

STEEL BRIDGE WITH BOTH DECKS RAISED

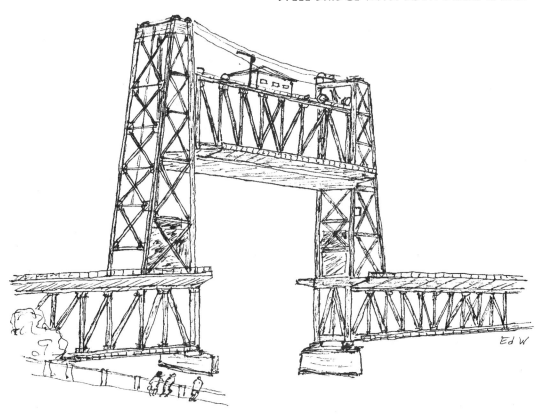

About the 1912 Steel Bridge: An incredible example of early twentieth century bridge design, the Steel Bridge is unique—the only double-deck bridge where the operator can lift the bottom deck (railroad/pedestrian/bicyclists) alone—without stopping traffic on the top deck (highway/MAX/pedestrians/bicyclists)—or lift both decks at once, moving up 90 feet in 90 seconds, displacing nine million pounds. The first Steel Bridge, opened in 1888, was also built by a railroad. A swing bridge, it had two decks, the upper deck for people, farm animals, and horse-drawn carriages; the bottom for freight trains. (A swing bridge, one of three movable bridge types, along with vertical lift and bascule, opens by rotating its span on a center pier located in the waterway.) The city wouldn't allow the 1888 bridge's construction unless it accommodated non-railroad users. The extant Steel Bridge turns 100 years old in 2012. For more about the Steel Bridge, see pp. 39–44 in *The Portland Bridge Book.*

14. Get off the MAX at the first station on the east side of the river. Depending on which color train you are riding, this will either be Rose Quarter or Interstate, the two stations across North Interstate Ave. from each other.

15. Turn south, toward downtown and the southeast side of the Steel Bridge; walk two blocks along either Interstate or Wheeler St. No matter which street you choose, you'll pass the Eastside Big Pipe Steel Bridge shaft, part of the $1 billion project to prevent untreated sewage from spilling into the Willamette River during rainstorms, as it does now.

16. Cross the intersection of Interstate and NE Oregon St. to get to the southeast end of the bridge.

17. Stay on the sidewalk, walking by verbena, red-orange begonia, purple pansies, and grass sculpted into a living peace sign.

Eastbank Esplanade Railroad Overcrossing Bridge

18. Follow the sidewalk down ten steps to the Railroad Overcrossing Bridge, an 80-foot-long Warren Truss. There is an overlook at the west end of the bridge providing a grand view of the west side.

> The tallest buildings in Portland are the U.S. Bancorp Tower, also known as "Big Pink," and the Wells Fargo Tower, the two bookending the skyline. The Bancorp Tower, 111 SW Fifth Ave., is 42 stories and 536 feet tall. Wells Fargo Tower, 1300 NW Fifth Ave., is 43 stories and stands 544 feet. By comparison, the tallest building in Seattle has 77 stories. The 13-story green glass building just south of the Steel Bridge is One Pacific Square/Northwest Natural Building, where this trip began.

19. Walk down another 52 steps, or take the ramp, and you're on the Eastbank Esplanade.

Options: Eastbank Esplanade Floating Bridge, Interpretive Signs

▶ From here you can turn left (south) on the Eastbank Esplanade. Just around the corner is a 1,200-foot-long floating bridge, designed by Tommy Rutherford of KPFF Engineering, the only female engineer, so far, to design a bridge on the Willamette River.

▶ South of the floating bridge you come to the east ends of the Burnside, Morrison, and Hawthorne bridges. All are accessible from the Eastbank Esplanade. The Burnside Bridge is getting its wheelchair lift replaced with an elevator in the

near future. The replacement does not interfere with walkers getting up to the
Burnside's highway deck from the Esplanade.

▶ Interpretive panels along the Esplanade include photographs and drawings of
the construction of the Steel Bridge, as well as a drawing of the one-mile Port-
land Harbor Wall, which is like an iceberg in that you can see only a small part
of its mass. The wall sits on 51 submerged timber cribs filled with gravel and
rocks, each crib 100 feet long by 37 feet high. For more about the Harbor Wall,
see p. 57.

Continuing the Basic Itinerary
Across the Bottom (Railroad) Deck of the Steel Bridge
and Over Some of the Oldest Exposed Dirt in Portland

20. On the way to the Steel Bridge, you pass a gravelly bank (on the left). This
is, in geology terms, Troutdale formation: earth laid down as flood deposits two
to ten million years ago, and some of the oldest dirt of its type in the Portland

area. This pebbly overhang (seen best looking back from the center of the Steel Bridge) is one of the few places in downtown, on either side of the river, not filled in by development since Europeans began expanding Portland in the mid-1840s. Troutdale formation is sometimes called God's concrete, because of its density and hardness.

EASTBANK ESPLANADE AT THE STEEL BRIDGE AND
TROUTDALE FORMATION—OLDEST EXPOSED DIRT
ALONG DOWNTOWN PORTLAND'S WATERFRONT

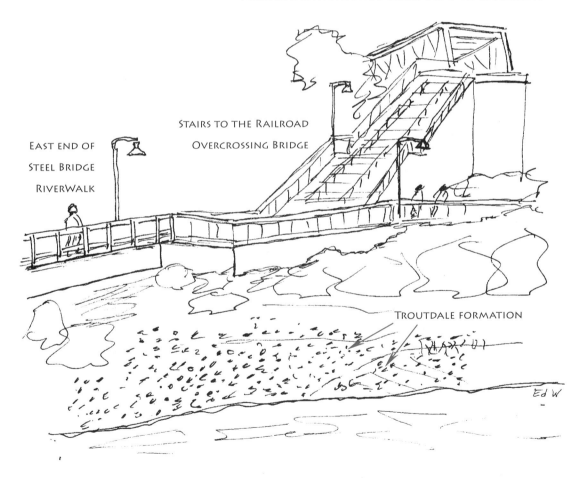

STAIRS TO THE RAILROAD
OVERCROSSING BRIDGE

EAST END OF
STEEL BRIDGE
RIVERWALK

TROUTDALE FORMATION

Ed W

Things to See at the Steel Bridge

21. Walk across the Steel Bridge on the sidewalk connecting with the Eastbank Esplanade.

That small white building halfway up the Steel Bridge's 245-foot-tall east end tower is the bridge operator's outhouse.

OPERATOR'S OUTHOUSE—EAST END TOWER OF THE STEEL BRIDGE

When the bridge operator, suspended below the wheel house on the top deck (in the marsupial position), needs to open the bottom deck, only 26 feet above water, you'll hear his warning over the public address system. The gates at both ends of the pedestrian walkway on the center span will close and you do not want to be on the wrong side of the gate.

There are two sets of security cameras, one at each end of the bottom deck lift span. The train deck is monitored in the Traffic Management Operation Center at the Oregon Department of Transportation.

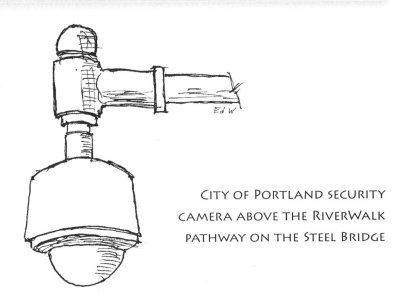

CITY OF PORTLAND SECURITY CAMERA ABOVE THE RIVERWALK PATHWAY ON THE STEEL BRIDGE

The $2.5 million cantilevered RiverWalk sidewalk on Steel's bottom deck was built in 2001 as part of the $31 million Esplanade. Pedestrians and bicyclists can also use the top deck, but RiverWalk ties the northern ends of the Esplanade and Waterfront Park together at the same elevation. Don't be surprised by the Amtrak trains and freight trains that cross the bottom deck of the bridge several times a day. The loud rumblings you hear overhead are the MAX trains, more than 400 trains a day, crossing the Steel Bridge every five to seven minutes each way, and more than 700 TriMet buses.

Looking to the east from the center of the Steel Bridge, you get a clear view of the Troutdale, the Railroad Overcrossing Bridge, Eastbank Esplanade Floating Bridge, and the east side sewer outfalls, the latter much visited by gulls when it's raining and sewage is pouring into the river. The outfall problem will be alleviated when the Big Pipe sewer project is finished in 2011. The system on the west side of the river is done.

22. Continue walking west 50 feet or so, past the two tall Lee Kelly sculptures on the left in the middle of the Friendship Circle at the northern end of Waterfront Park.

23. Turn right (north) on the sidewalk adjacent to Naito.

Willamette Greenway Trail and McCormick Pier: in the Working Part of Portland Harbor

24. Walk across the double main line tracks of the Union Pacific Railroad, seeing the Steel Bridge's bottom deck on your right (east). Looking west, you see the historic train station, three blocks away, where you will soon arrive for a restroom break.

25. Where the sidewalk splits just north of the railroad tracks, bear right, toward the river. Pass a "Willamette Greenway Trail" sign, on your left. The Greenway is the sidewalk between McCormick Pier condominiums and apartments and the Willamette River. Built in 1980 by Bill Naito, McCormick Pier extends to the Broadway Bridge, one-third of a mile north of the Steel Bridge.

26. Walk one block on the Greenway. If the Willamette is low enough between the boat dock and a large flagpole on the edge of the Greenway, you'll see what looks like the piers from the west end of the 1888 Steel (swing) Bridge. Cormorants like to perch on top of the piers by the boat dock.

27. Keep going, past steps leading into McCormick Pier and, on the right, stone steps leading to the riprapped beach and a Fido House, equipped with plastic bags.

28. Stop near the tall steel light standard and corner post of a large concrete seating area (both to the left of the Greenway) and a piece of chain-link fence on your right (east), which prevents people from falling off the sidewalk into the Willamette. When the river is low, you'll see a square wooden base protruding from the edge of the river—this is where the McCormick Pier Gazebo stood until one of the legs broke in 2007, tipping 50 structural engineers, a couple of sturgeon fishermen, and one guide farther toward the river than they wanted to be. A 25-foot-long aluminum walkway connected the sidewalk/Greenway to the gazebo.

29. At the standard, turn left (west) off the Greenway and walk through the paved area, built in 2005 for pedestrians and bicyclists to get from the waterfront through McCormick Pier to Naito.

30. On this short half-block uphill walk to Naito, you'll pass between train sheds converted to parking garages.

Options: the Broadway Bridge, Albers Mill, and the Frank Ivancie Footbridge

▶ Do not turn toward Naito, but continue north on the Greenway Trail another one-third of a mile, crossing under the deck of the Broadway Bridge. On the left (west) will be the bridge's Pier IV, built on a deep caisson.

About the Broadway Bridge: Opened in 1913, it carries Broadway between NW Portland and NE Portland. Its bascule span counterweights are located above the roadway rather than inside the river piers as on the Morrison and Burnside bridges. Broadway's river piers sit on pneumatic caissons, which were dug into the river bottom by crews working inside in compressed air. The Pier IV caisson next to the Greenway footbridge was one of the deepest pneumatic caissons in the U.S. when constructed. The bottom of the concrete-filled timber caisson sits 85 feet below the surface of the Willamette. The operator works on the northwest corner of the bascule span. The Broadway Bridge turns 100 years old in 2013. (For more about the Broadway Bridge and caissons, see pp. 31–38 and p. 170 in the third edition of *The Portland Bridge Book*.)

Also under the Broadway Bridge is the Frank Ivancie Footbridge, cantilevered over the river where it connects the Greenway to the ocean-sized wooden dock at Albers Mill, 1200 NW Naito Pkwy. Named for a Portland mayor (1980–1984), the footbridge opened in 1992 and extended the Greenway to NW Ninth Ave. Albers Mill, opened as a mill in 1911, is now the headquarters for wheat industry planners. The wooden dock to the north of the building provides a spectacular view of the Fremont Bridge, another half mile north.

Continuing the Basic Itinerary
Two Blocks to Union Station

31. After walking through McCormick Pier, cross Naito to the sidewalk and 26 steps that lead to the courtyard at the Yards at Union Station Apartment complex, 815 NW Naito Pkwy. The courtyard ends at the steps leading to the Union Station Pedestrian Bridge.

> Built by the Portland Development Commission (PDC) for the Housing Authority of Portland in 1998, the Yards sit on property abandoned in the 1970s by the Burlington Northern Railroad and located on a brownfield. Total petroleum hydrocarbons (TPHs), polynucleur aromatic hydrocarbons (PAHs), lead and arsenic, and crude oil contaminates were capped in a plan approved by the Oregon Department of Environmental Quality prior to development.

32. Before taking the steps, look north along Naito and you'll see the red metal stairway at the southwest end of the Broadway Bridge.

Union Station Pedestrian Bridge

33. Climb the steps to the courtyard of the Yards at Union Station and you'll see the Union Station Pedestrian Bridge and its stairway and elevator.

> About the Union Station Pedestrian Bridge: This steel tied arch opened in 2000 to carry pedestrians and bicyclists over the railroad tracks at Portland Union Station, proving once again that bridges are always solutions to problems. Built to emulate the Fremont Bridge (seen to the north), it is criticized by some for not fitting in architecturally with the historic train station buildings, listed on the National Register. It is, however, extremely flexible and an excellent place to excite the molecules.

COACH

Ed W

Test for Synchronous Vertical Excitation

34. Whether alone or with others, you may want to consider conducting a test for synchronous vertical excitation and the more weight you can muster, the merrier the molecules. This means walking on the bridge until you're standing under the arch. Count to three and then jump as high as you can without hurting yourself. With only a little flexing of the knees the excitement can go on for a long time.

From the Union Station Bridge, in addition to the Fremont and Broadway bridges, you can see the Greyhound Bus terminal, with its steel cable-hung roof and, according to some travelers, one of the nicer Greyhound depots in the U.S.

GREYHOUND DEPOT'S
CABLE-HUNG ROOF

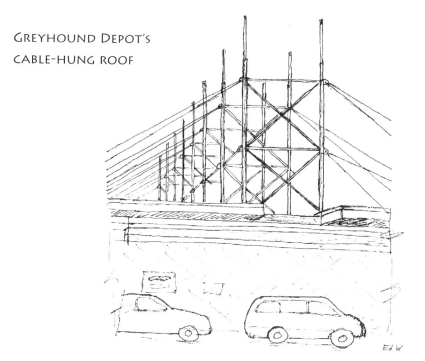

The small, two-story brick building with small white crosses on its façade farther south along the tracks is the VC Tower, named for its FCC-assigned call letters. Also called the Interlocking Tower and Switch Tower, it was built in 1914 and abandoned in 1997 by the Portland Terminal Railroad Co. This is where the telegrapher who copied the train orders and the tower man who pulled the levers to switch the trains worked. After photocopying and facsimile machines were invented, telegraphy became obsolete. The tower closed completely when switching here went from manual to computerized operation. (Train handling for the Union Pacific is controlled from Omaha, Nebraska, while the BNSF controls its track from St. Louis, Missouri.) The switching and telegraphy equipment in VC Tower was removed in October 2007. TriMet has now leased the building for its expanded MAX operations in NW Portland.

UNION TRAIN STATION VC TOWER

35. At the west end of the Union Station Pedestrian Bridge, walk down 41 steps or take the elevator and you'll be on the sidewalk leading to the front door of Union Station, 800 NW Sixth Ave.

Portland Union Station and Fossils from the Jurassic Period

36. Portland Union Station is open seven days a week, 7:30 a.m.–8:45 p.m. This National Register building, dedicated February 14, 1896, is treasured for its location, clock tower, flowered ceiling, drinking fountains, old scenic murals, and the

very large, clean, warm bathrooms open to the public. The limestone walls of the room leading to the bathrooms invite a closer look: embedded in the limestone are shark teeth and other ammonites (fossils) from the Jurassic period (206 to 144 million years ago). What's not so obvious is that Union Station sits on submerged timber piling. This land, all fill, was once the site of Couch Lake and when it rains, the lawn in and around the rose beds outside get extra boggy. In the mid-1980s, PDC assumed ownership of Union Station and a much-needed renovation again. Also see Exploration Five "Amtrak from Portland, Oregon, All the Way to Vancouver, Washington Over Three Movable Bridges—And Back."

UNION STATION CLOCK TOWER

37. To finish up Exploration Two, walk two blocks east and three blocks south to NW Fourth Ave. and Everett, an easier task once MAX construction finishes.

End Point, NW Second and Everett

38. Turn left on Everett and walk two blocks to Second and you'll be back where you started. Keep an eye out for Chinatown's five-bay gate, across West Burnside at NW Fourth Ave, one of the largest China Gates in the U.S. The red lampposts in Chinatown (six blocks long and two blocks wide) came from the SW Morrison Street right-of-way along the MAX alignment. When MAX construction took out the posts in 1986, Portlanders, famous for recycling, re-painted them red and re-erected them to mark Chinatown's boundaries.

Recommendations for Lunch

In Chinatown, I recommend the Golden Horse Restaurant, 238 NW Fourth Ave. at Everett. The Portland Classical Chinese Garden's teahouse, 127 NW Third Ave., also serves lunch.

Continuing north just across West Burnside, you'll find Dan & Louis Oyster Bar, 208 SW Ankeny St. This is Portland's second oldest restaurant; Huber's, 411 SW Third Ave., is the oldest. At Dan & Louis you'll find hundreds and hundreds of plates, photographs, and other priceless artifacts relating to early Portland history. One photo shows the city during the 1894 flood, with people rowing boats through the blocks where this exploration started.

Keeping it Going:
Boarding TriMet #8 for the Veterans Hospital Skybridge and the Portland Aerial Tram

Rather than returning to Second and Everett, you could board TriMet Bus #8 at Third and Flanders, arriving at the Veterans Hospital, at the other end of Portland, in 22–25 minutes. Here you could walk across the Veterans Hospital Skybridge and ride downhill on the Portland Aerial Tram. See Exploration Three "A Free Ride on the Bridge That's the Portland Aerial Tram."

La Pine Middle Schoolers
Encounter Portland Sidewalk Weather

The population there worried
about forest fires, but here
we sweat not the hurricanes
plaguing Florida,
earthquakes unsettling Anchorage,
twisters lifting Kansas.
Our natural worry is flood,
the rain lately slumping the earth
to her knees like the converted
come to Jesus.
Current predictions call
for coastal tsunamis to rise
fast as the heron—the bird
we spot today paddling
its ocean-blue wings between
the balconies of office buildings
at the corner of SW Third and Taylor,
long legs forming a single rudder
as we, waders of concrete,
hold our noses against
the smell of what floats pasts us
in the wake of today's lost
and displaced: human excrement,
condoms, semi-digested spaghetti
and meatballs hurled up the stairs
along Morrison's west end railing—
But not for the moment we look up,
point at the fragile heron
surviving this low-bottom city.—SWW

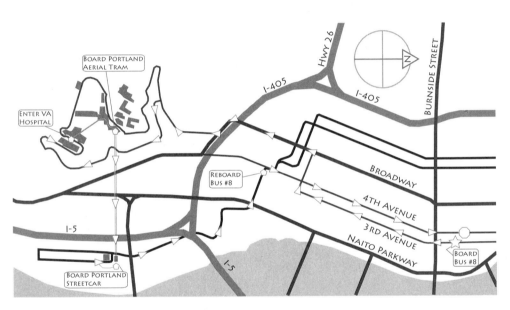

Note: This map shows returning to the starting point in Old Town by #8 bus along SW Fourth Ave. The instructions on p. 88 (Step 8) suggest staying on the Portland Streetcar to SW Tenth and Yamhill, then crossing the street and catching any MAX eastbound to return to the starting point. Either way works.

Exploration Three

A Free Ride on the Bridge that's the Portland Aerial Tram

This loop, all by public transportation, begins and ends in Old Town.

▶ Walk across the Veterans Administration Medical Center Skybridge, the longest air-conditioned pedestrian bridge in the United States.

▶ Visit Oregon Health & Science University's Kohler Pavilion Overlook (adjacent to the upper terminal of the Portland Aerial Tram) for a ninth floor view of Mt. Hood, a then-and-now interpretive panel of the SE and SW waterfront and the Willamette River, and a drink of Bull Run water from the bronze bird-shaped fountains of sculptors Frank Boyden and Brad Rude.

▶ Ride the Portland Aerial Tram from Pill Hill (the nickname for the medical enclave in Portland's southwest hills) to South Waterfront, Portland's newest neighborhood, located between the Ross Island Bridge and the Old Spaghetti Factory.

➤ For an elevated look at the Ross Island Bridge and Zidell Marine Corporation's barge building operations, visit the 16th floor overlook on the top floor of OHSU's Center for Health & Healing, the latter just south of the tram's lower terminal (optional).

➤ Before returning to Downtown, eat at the Daily Café or the Old Spaghetti Factory (optional).

➤ To extend this exploration, and depending on the season, board the Willamette Shore Trolley at the southern end of South Waterfront for a 5.5-mile ride to Lake Oswego to see Frank Boyden's Stafford Stones in Foothills Park (optional).

➤ Returning to Portland from South Waterfront on the Portland Streetcar, transfer to Metropolitan Area Express (MAX) light rail at SW Tenth and Yamhill for a one-mile ride to Old Town.

Basics

Distance: Four miles (one way) from Old Town to the Portland Aerial Tram.

Time: Old Town to Old Town, with limited stops, 90 minutes. The-Get-Off-and-On-and-Looking-Around-Itinerary takes 1–½ to 2 hours, plus any side trips.

Parking in Old Town: Smart Park Garage, NW First Ave. and Davis (entrance on Davis); one block east of the Old Town/Chinatown MAX Station and near the northern end of the Portland Transit Mall.

Hours for the Portland Aerial Tram: Monday-Friday 6:00 a.m.–10 p.m., Saturday 9:00 a.m.–5:00 p.m., closed on Sundays.

Hours for the Center for Health & Healing 16th floor clinics (South Waterfront): Weekdays except Wednesday, 8:00 a.m.–5:00 p.m.; Wednesday 9:15 a.m.–5:00 p.m.; closed weekends.

Hours for the Old Spaghetti Factory, 0715 SW Bancroft: Weekdays except Friday, 11:30 a.m.–2:30 p.m. and 4:30 p.m.–9:30 p.m. Friday 11:30 a.m.–2:30 p.m. and 4:30 p.m.–10:30 p.m. Saturday 12:30–10:30 p.m. Sunday 12:30–9:30 p.m.

Fare (tram): There is no charge for riding the tram downhill. A ticket ($4 in 2007) is only required for the ride uphill.

Fare (bus): The city is divided into three bus zones. Where you travel determines your fare. Old Town to the tram is in Zone 1, or $1.75 for adults, 85 cents for seniors, and $1.40 for youth. Save the transfer the driver gives you at the time of boarding; it's good for two hours on the streetcar, MAX, or another bus.

School groups: Board TriMet's #8 bus as far north on the transit mall as possible, since fewer people will be on the bus, allowing more room for students.

Refreshments: You'll pass three espresso stands on your way from the VA Skybridge to the Kohler Pavilion. The Daily Café, in the first floor of the Center for Health & Healing (at the tram's lower terminal), serves weekdays. You can always get sidetracked by the Old Spaghetti Factory, or take a picnic lunch and eat on the benches overlooking the river on the Willamette Greenway just south (right) of the Old Spaghetti Factory.

Site Specifics

▶ Pill Hill is home to four major medical institutions: OHSU, Shriners Hospital for Children, Doernbecher Children's Hospital, and the Veterans Administration Hospital.

➤ Part of the 409-acre North Macadam Urban Renewal Area, South Waterfront is a new Portland neighborhood developing south of the Ross Island Bridge, located at Willamette River mile 14. In 1999, the Portland City Council voted to develop this site, formerly zoned industrial, extending the Central City District. Plans included new housing, employment, walking paths, parks, trails, light rail, and an aerial tram.

➤ Maxed out for space at higher elevations, OHSU funded most of the construction costs of the tram and continues to contribute to its annual maintenance. The tram is the bridge that made it feasible for OHSU to expand into South Waterfront. The first OHSU building to finish in South Waterfront is the Center for Health & Healing, 3303 SW Bond Ave., just to the south of the tram's lower landing. For more about OHSU see p. 85. For more about South Waterfront, go to <www.pdc.us/>.

<---------->

TriMet Bus to the VA Hospital Skybridge

1. Catch #8 bus on the Portland Transit Mall (runs every 15 minutes) to the entrance of the VA Hospital, 3710 SW Veterans Hospital Rd. The land here was donated in 1926, with the extant hospital opened in 1988. The Cancer Research Center, the newest building on the VA campus, opened in 1999.

2. Using the stairs or elevators beyond the front door of the VA Hospital, go up one flight to the second floor and the entrance to the 660-foot-long skybridge. The skybridge connects the VA Hospital to the ninth floor of OHSU Hospital South.

Option

You can bypass the VA Hospital and skybridge, getting off the #8 TriMet bus at the front door of the Kohler Pavilion, 3181 SW Sam Jackson Park Rd., which is closer to the tram's upper entrance than the skybridge route.

Continuing the Basic Intinerary:

3. Cross the skybridge, notice off to your right (northeast) the tram's upper terminal and arriving and departing tramcars. To the left (northwest) of the skybridge is Doernbecher, built in the shape of a bridge across Campus Drive.

> About the VA Skybridge: Opened in 1992, this $6.8 million combination truss and cable-stayed bridge is supported by two towers anchored in a 150-foot-deep ravine. Purported to be the longest air-conditioned pedestrian bridge in the world (660 feet long or two football fields), it connects the VA Hospital on one end and OHSU Hospital South on the other. The bridge has eliminated the need for long ambulance rides through the canyon between the two institutions and almost immediately paid for itself. For more about the skybridge, see p. 179 in the third edition of *The Portland Bridge Book*.

VETERANS ADMINISTRATION HOSPITAL SKYBRIDGE

Ed W

About the tram: Opened in 2006 at a cost of $57 million, the tram is Portland's newest and most exotic form of public transportation. It carries commuters between the city's South Waterfront district and the OHSU campus. The tram is actually two cars, named *Jean* and *Walt*, after Jean Richardson, the first female engineering graduate from Oregon State University, and Walt Reynolds, the first African-American to graduate from OHSU. *Jean* and *Walt* alternate, departing from the ninth floor of the Kohler Center every five minutes with up to 78 passengers (maximum carrying capacity, plus the operator). Riders travel 3,300 feet in two minutes 50 seconds, crossing four major highways (Terwilliger Blvd., Barbur Blvd., Macadam Ave., and I-5), qualifying the tram as a bridge. There are three major structures for the tram: the upper terminal, at OHSU; the lower terminal, at South Waterfront on SW Gibbs St.; and the intermediate tower, east of I-5. The latter is 197 feet tall. The original architectural plans called for a wooden tower, but the forces were too high for wood—made of steel, this tower is designed to withstand one million pounds of side pull. For more about the tram go to <www.portlandtram.org/>.

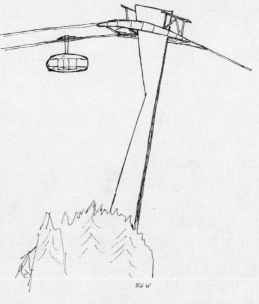

TRAM AND INTERMEDIATE TOWER

OHSU Hospital South

4. There is a tram sign in the ceiling above the espresso stand at the OHSU end of the skybridge. Follow the signs through the halls of Hospital South to the Kohler Center and the tram's entrance.

PORTLAND AERIAL TRAM SIGNS IN
OREGON HEALTH & SCIENCE UNIVERSITY
SOUTH AND THE KOHLER CENTER

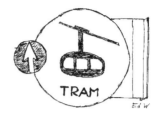

About OHSU: The 116-acre Marquam Hill campus originated in 1914 with a 20-acre tract of land donated by the Oregon-Washington Railroad & Navigation Co. Today the Marquam Hill campus is connected to OHSU's new Center for Health & Healing in the South Waterfront District via the tram. Plans are underway to develop an additional campus adjacent to South Waterfront in the years to come. Other recent expansion includes the Kohler Pavilion and the Biomedical Research Building, built for $346 million. OHSU is Portland's largest employer with about 12,500 employees. The only health and research university in Oregon, it annually educates 3,500 students and trainees; is visited by more than 750,000 patients; and conducts more than 4,000 research projects. OHSU occupies more than six million square feet of space in 36 buildings. The public artwork, 800 pieces tucked in and about Marquam Hill, is impressive. To help you navigate, there are now seven concierge stations, including one each at the upper tram entrance and near the lower tram terminal in the Center for Health & Healing. To speak to the head concierge, call 503-494-8311 and ask for the station at OHSU Hospital South.

Portland Aerial Tram

5. Across from the Kohler Pavilion concierge's desk and public restrooms is a nine-story high outdoor overlook with a dead-on view of Mt. Hood, about 50 miles east.

An interpretive panel on the overlook compares the Portland we can see in the distance to Portland as it looked before any bridges spanned the lower Willamette, or pre-1887. Artists Frank Boyden and Brad Rude created two bronze fountains, a water feature, and two slab benches, also on the overlook. (The two collaborated on the fabulous lobby, vestibule, and entrance circle of Doernbecher when it opened in 1998.) For more about Boyden's work see p. 89.

BOYDEN-RUDE FOUNTAIN
AND INTERPRETIVE PANEL
KOHLER OVERLOOK

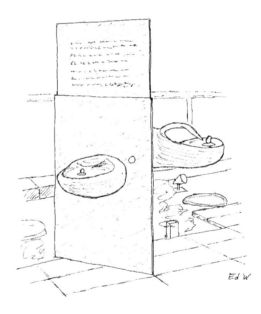

6. Board the tram, a car departing every five minutes. You will land at the lower terminal in less than three minutes. Remember, there is no charge for riding downhill.

OHSU Center for Health & Healing Rooftop View

7. Depending on the time of your visit, it's possible to take the elevator to the 16th floor of the Center for Health & Healing, 3303 SW Bond Ave. (see p. 81 for the Center's hours). From the rooftop overlook or from the tram, you can see several landmarks. If the door is locked to the overlook (usually due to wind), check with the receptionist in the Dermatology Clinic for a key.

The Ross Island Bridge: Opened in 1926, Ross Island looks like an arch bridge, but is actually a cantilever truss, and carries drinking water from the Bull Run Reservoir in pipes running along its length, making it an aqueduct, a tall aqueduct—123 feet clearance between the structure and the Willamette. Ross Island is one of three bridges from Gustav Lindenthal, the famous New York City bridge engineer, who also designed the Sellwood Bridge (1925), and completed construction of the Burnside Bridge (1926). For more about the Ross Island Bridge and cantilever trusses, see pp. 75–82 and p. 160 in *The Portland Bridge Book*.

Zidell Marine: In operation for almost a century, Zidell builds ocean-going barges, some more than 300 feet long, just north of the tram's lower landing.

The John Ross Center, the 323-foot-tall condominium to the south of the Health and Healing Center, is the tallest building in South Waterfront. The penthouse, 5,000 square feet, reportedly sold for $5 million in 2007.

8. To return to Old Town, board either the southbound or northbound Portland Streetcar at the tram's lower terminal at SW Gibbs St. and Moody Ave. (Weekdays, the streetcar picks up and drops off every 13 minutes.) The streetcar makes three more stops farther south before returning to Gibbs and Moody and the ten-minute ride to SW Tenth and Yamhill (Library Station) where you get off the streetcar to transfer to MAX for the ride to Old Town.

About the Portland Streetcar: Ten cars (manufactured in the Czech Republic) pick up and drop off at 42 stops in a continuous 7.2-mile loop between NW 23rd Ave., and SW Lowell St. and Bond Ave. The latter station is located two blocks north and west of the Old Spaghetti Factory, which sits on the banks of the Willamette River at the southern perimeter of South Waterfront. Each streetcar carries up to 140 passengers, and runs about every 13 minutes most weekdays. For fares and hours of operation, go to <www.portlandstreetcar.org>.

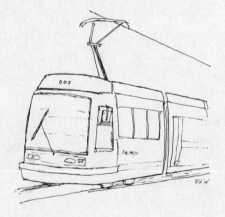

End of the Line Options

▶ The Willamette Shore Trolley, depending on the time of year, can extend the Portland Aerial Tram-South Waterfront-Portland Streetcar experience. The WST's Bancroft St. Station is two blocks from the Old Spaghetti Factory, and only a block from the streetcar's last stop in South Waterfront at the SW Lowell St. and Bond Ave. Station. In a 40-minute, 5.5-mile ride along the Willamette River to Lake Oswego, riders pass through 1,396-foot Elk Rock Tunnel (with an "S" curve between its portals, the mid-section of the tunnel in complete darkness) and over several trestles, including the 686-foot-long Riverwood Trestle.

▶ Within walking distance of WST's Lake Oswego Station, 311 N. State St. (near A St.), you'll find more Frank Boyden sculptures. Nine-acre Foothills Park, once a wood chip-making plant, was dedicated April 19, 2006. Boyden sculpted lines of William Stafford poetry into towering polished basalt pillars positioned to be touched and read. (The park is also served by TriMet bus #31 and has plenty of free parking for vehicles.) From WST's Lake Oswego Station, walk through the opening in the chain-link fence, then straight ahead to Oswego Pt. Dr. Turn left (north) on Foothills Dr. toward the Willamette River. All the streets are well marked. It is one-third mile from the trolley to the stones, located in the north end of the park. For more about the WST and its fares and schedule, go to <www.trainweb.org/oerhs/wst>. For more about William Stafford, see this book's table of contents, or go to <www.williamstafford.org>.

The Third Grade Tour

All of them fresher than new sticks of gum,
they spread out with me on sidewalks
this city bears down on.

The ones most uncontainable
worry their way to the front,
to talk in my one good ear

they bend back and forth
with the hard stuff at home
I don't want to hear about.

The questions, too, arrive heavy,
heavy as wooden bedposts:
Is it okay to spit?

Are there bats down there?
What exactly is a bascule pit?
My dad calls every Sunday

but sometimes he doesn't mean
to forget. Will we see any
pelicans? Will the tram snap?

I say, Stick with me, Kid.
We're going to unwrap this morning
like it's a sweet tooth.—SWW

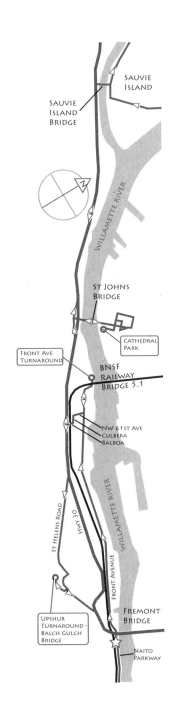

SAUVIE
ISLAND

SAUVIE
ISLAND
BRIDGE

WILLAMETTE RIVER

ST JOHNS
BRIDGE

CATHEDRAL
PARK

FRONT AVE
TURNAROUND

BNSF
RAILWAY
BRIDGE 5.1

NW 61ST AVE
CULBERA
BALBOA

ST HELENS ROAD

HWY 30

WILLAMETTE RIVER

FRONT AVENUE

UPSHUR
TURNAROUND –
BALCH GULCH
BRIDGE

FREMONT
BRIDGE

NAITO
PARKWAY

☆	START
—	ROUTE
▥	RAILROAD
▷	DIRECTION
○	FINISH

Exploration Four

FROM THE (REPAIRED) CRACK IN THE FREMONT BRIDGE TO THE
BURLINGTON NORTHERN SANTA FE RAILWAY BRIDGE 5.1 TO THE ST. JOHNS
BRIDGE TO THE SAUVIE ISLAND BRIDGE TO THE HANGING DECK TRUSS
CARRYING NW THURMAN ST. OVER BALCH GULCH

This drive-around begins and ends at the Fremont Bridge. In the industrial/port/railroad part of the city, see Portland's:

➤ Longest bridge: Fremont, owned by the Oregon Dept. of Transportation;

➤ Most modified bridge: Burlington Northern Santa Fe Railway Bridge 5.1, owned by BNSF Railway Co.;

➤ Most elegant bridge: St. Johns, owned by ODOT;

➤ Newest bridge: Sauvie Island, owned by Multnomah County;

➤ Oldest bridge: Balch Gulch, owned by the City of Portland.

Basics

Distance: 25 miles round-trip
Time: About two hours in a motorized vehicle, longer by bicycle or on foot
Bridges Visited: Five

Site Specifics

About the Port of Portland and marine activities: In 1891, the Oregon legislature created the Port of Portland to dredge a shipping channel from Portland to the Pacific Ocean. The Port now owns four marine terminals, four airports, and seven business parks. It also owns and operates the dredge *Oregon*. In 2004, ocean-going vessels on the navigational channel between Kelley Point and the Pacific transported $16 billion worth of U.S. goods to and from world markets. The Willamette's export contributions include fertilizers, soda ash, iron and steel, and grain, a lot of grain. Columbia Grain Inc. at Terminal 5 (1550 N. Lombard St.) has a rapid-handling grain elevator where almost four million short tons of grain were handled in 2006. The grain comes from farms in eastern Oregon and Idaho. It is barged to Portland from the Port of Lewiston and exported to such countries as Japan, Egypt, Philippines, South Korea, Taiwan, Singapore, Indonesia, Thailand, Chile, and Ecuador. This marine enterprise has existed here since the first shipment of wheat left Portland docks in 1863 bound for England. In addition to being the largest wheat-exporting region in North America, the Columbia and Willamette River system is also the third largest grain export region in the world. Recently, the vessel *Armstrong* took on 25,000 tons of white wheat (bound for Pakistan) at the "O" Dock Elevator, just north of the Steel Bridge.

To accommodate ever-bigger vessels, six lower river ports petitioned the U.S. Army Corps of Engineers to deepen the navigation channel by three feet. The sponsor ports in Oregon are Portland and St. Helens. This was not an idea loved by everybody. Even so, dredging to deepen 103.5 miles of the Columbia River channel began in June 2005. In the first year, the U.S. Army Corps of Engineers' dredging contractor and the Port of Portland's dredge *Oregon* deepened 28 miles of the channel from 40 to 43 feet. The total cost is expected to run $150.5 million, or about $1.5 million a mile for all 103.5 miles.

The federal navigation channel in the Willamette stretches from the Broadway Bridge in Portland downstream to the Columbia River. According to the Port of Portland, the Corps is now preparing a dredged material management plan (DMMP) for the existing 40-foot deep Lower Willamette River navigation channel. The DMMP will be a 20-year plan for managing material dredged from the channel to maintain its authorized depth and provide safe navigation. The Corps last dredged the Willamette's channel in 1997. Historically, the Corps dredged between 500,000 and 750,000 cubic yards of sediment from the channel every three to five years. However, the Corps deferred channel maintenance when the U.S. Environmental Protection Agency listed the Portland Harbor as a Superfund site in December 2000. Superfund is, according to the U.S. Environmental Protection Agency, a name given to the program established to reclaim abandoned hazardous waste sites. It's also the name of the fund established as a result of a 1980 law enacted in the wake of the discovery of toxic waste dumps such as Love Canal (New York), and Times Beach (Missouri) in the 1970s. Part of the Willamette's flood plain was designated a National Natural Landmark in 1987 and the river itself was named an American Heritage River in 1997. For more about the Port of Portland see <www.portofportland.com> and for more about the Willamette's Superfund status see <www.willamette-riverkeeper.org/super1.htm>. Also see Exploration Two "Three Bridge Walk" for more about the Willamette River.

Orientation

From its beginning high in the Cascades south and east of Eugene, the Willamette River follows a northerly route through the Willamette Valley. When it gets to Portland, it jogs northwest as it heads to Kelley Point and the Columbia River. The bridges between the Eastbank Esplanade and Tom McCall Waterfront Park in the Central City mostly run east to west, but just before the Steel Bridge, the river makes a 45-degree curve to the west, putting the Steel, Broadway, Fremont, and BNSF 5.1 bridges on a northeast to southwest alignment. The St. Johns Bridge, located at a peninsula, also runs northeast to southwest. People here, with North Portland addresses, know everything else in Portland as south of their location. When asked for directions, many position themselves as north of the St. Johns Bridge, instead of on the east side of the Willamette.

Hemmed in by the Willamette River and the Tualatin Mountains (West Hills), Portland's central business district, about six miles upriver from the St. Johns Bridge, sits on one square mile. The growing city had nowhere to expand but north, east, and south—today 80 percent of Portland's population lives on the east side of the Willamette River.

Repaired Crack on the Fremont Bridge
0.4 miles north of the Steel Bridge

1. Start at 1750 NW Naito Pkwy. Park in the lot between Naito and the Willamette River to walk around two of the Fremont Bridge's four 16-foot-tall

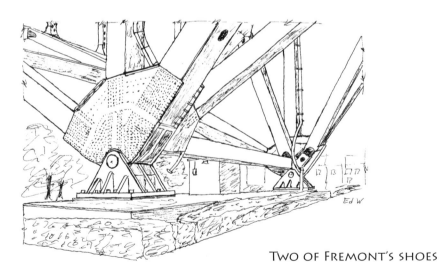

TWO OF FREMONT'S SHOES

bearings. Gravity pulls Fremont's 30,000 tons into the ground through these bearings (also called *footings* or *shoes*), two on the east side and two on the west side.

2. Standing at the parking lot curb, look up and you can see the patch in a section of the Fremont Bridge that cracked and threatened to fall across Naito in 1971.

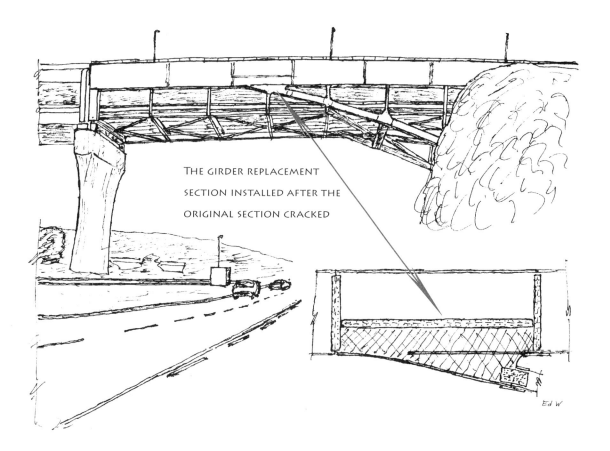

THE GIRDER REPLACEMENT
SECTION INSTALLED AFTER THE
ORIGINAL SECTION CRACKED

Ed W

(REPAIRED) CRACK IN THE FREMONT BRIDGE

About the Fremont Bridge: Its side spans were erected first, and after the cracking problem was fixed, the 6,000-ton center span, constructed at Swan Island, was floated upstream and lifted into place from barges in the Willamette River. This was the largest bridge lift in the world at the time. The Fremont Bridge opened in 1973 and remains the largest tied arch bridge in North America. Tied arch means the bridge is designed like an archer's bow, with the "string" (or tie) connecting one end to the other. Tied arches are used at sites where it is not feasible to support the arch horizontally at ground level. The tie carries the horizontal thrust that would otherwise be taken by canyon walls.

In the spring, you may see peregrine falcons, nesting on the Fremont Bridge since 1993. In its dive, the peregrine falcon is the fastest animal on earth. For more about the bridge and Portland's peregrines, see pp. 23–30 and p. 112 in the third edition in *The Portland Bridge Book*, and <www.audubonportland.org/livingwithwildlife/peregrines/pdx-peregrines>.

Next Stop: BNSF Railway Bridge 5.1
4.2 miles from the Fremont Bridge

3. Head north on Naito, which reverts to Front at the Fremont Bridge. Note that the waterfront on your right, formerly zoned industrial, is now filled with condominiums.

4. Also on your right, a little past 3660 NW First Ave. and north of the Port of Portland's Terminal 2 dock, is Engine House #6 where the historic fireboat *David Campbell* is tethered when not working the river or officially spraying environmentally friendly colored water to welcome Rose Festival ships.

The forested area off to your left is Forest Park. At 5,156.65 acres, it is, according to Portland Parks, the largest forested natural area within city limits in the United States. The St. Johns Bridge and the BNSF Railway Bridge 5.1 come into view at NW 61st Ave. and Front.

5. Continue on Front until it dead-ends, going past Gunderson (makers of rail cars and giant ocean-going barges), the Shell dock, Kittridge Ave. Bridge, and Metro's Central Transfer Station for waste collection and recycling.

6. The turnaround where Front dead-ends (just past BNSF's granite river piers) was constructed by TriMet and is public property. There is plenty of room to loop around, even for a school bus. As you do, you can easily view and photograph BNSF Railway Bridge 5.1. On the other side of the dead end is Siltronic Corp., 7200 Front, manufacturers of silicon wafers for the semiconductor industry. Siltronic takes its security seriously—the landscaped and grassy areas next to the public turnaround are, despite excellent views of Bridge 5.1, off limits to the public.

About BNSF Railway Bridge 5.1: The silver-colored spans date to 1908. The dark red, rust-colored vertical lift span is 516 feet long and made of weathering steel as is the 2007 Sauvie Island Bridge. The lift span replaced a swing-style span, deemed a hazard to navigation. The change took place in 1989. Because BNSF 5.1 is part of the railroad's main line, engineers and ironworkers had only 72 hours to replace the span and restore train service. Engineers do amazing things. The bridge's 1908 parts turn 100 years old in 2008; the lift span not until 2089. For more about BNSF Railway Bridge 5.1 see pp. 119–124 in the third edition of *The Portland Bridge Book*.

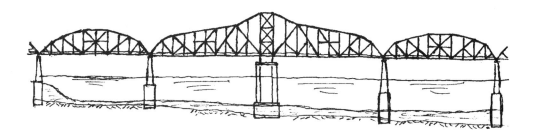

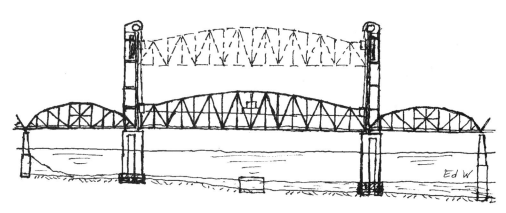

BURLINGTON NORTHERN SANTA FE RAILWAY BRIDGE 5.1, OLD AND NEW

Next Stop: St. Johns Bridge
Three miles from BNSF Railway Bridge 5.1

7. Backtrack on Front (traveling south 0.7 mile) to 61st.

8. Turn right, passing Metro's Central Transfer Station at 6161 NW 61st. 61st becomes Culebra Ave. as you curve left and then Balboa Ave. as you curve right.

9. Cross the main line of the BNSF Railway to NW St. Helens Rd.

10. Turn right on St. Helens (U.S. Highway 30).

11. Continue north following signs to the St. Johns Bridge.

12. Turn left at the stoplight and go up the hill on NW Bridge Ave. (unmarked).

The abandoned gray concrete building with the empty clock tower ahead on your right is part of the Portland Gas & Coke Company's Linnton Plant, which made gas from oil, not coal. Opened in 1913, this was an office building made to last: slate roof and poured concrete walls.

As you start up the approach to the St. Johns Bridge, notice that the bridge's suspension cables on the east side of the river go into the massive anchorage located in Cathedral Park. The cables on the west side are anchored in the basalt bluff under Forest Park.

St. Johns Bridge east end anchorage

Ed W

13. Turn right onto the bridge's main span, which is N. Philadelphia Ave. (also unmarked). This takes you through the St. Johns' Gothic towers.

> About the St. Johns Bridge: Opened in 1931 and now a Portland Historical Landmark, the bridge's cables were spun at the New Jersey plant of John A. Roebling's Sons Co., of Brooklyn Bridge (1883) fame. St. Johns is the only major suspension highway bridge in the Willamette Valley. For more about the St. Johns Bridge, see pp. 15–22 in the third edition of *The Portland Bridge Book*. To see large-scale photographs of the bridge under construction, see directions to the St. Johns Burgerville on p. 106 (under Options).

14. From the center span you can see, on your right, BNSF 5.1, Siltronics, the Fremont Bridge, and downtown Portland. On your left is the last of the Willamette River; only six miles downstream the Willamette meets the Columbia River. Downriver, too, is a large paved area known as Berth 415, or Terminal 4 Auto. This is the main Toyota dock where tall, boxy-shaped ships called car-carriers deliver hundreds and hundreds of Toyotas at a time.

15. At the east end of the bridge, just past the last section of the bridge's concrete light standards and railing, turn right on N. Syracuse St.

> The brick building here, formerly St. Johns City Hall, is now the Portland Police Department's North Precinct, 7214 N. Philadelphia. The St. Johns Heritage Association maintains files and glass cases with artifacts on the second floor. It is open the fourth Wednesday of the month 10:30 a.m.-noon. For more information, call SJHA at 503-621-3864, or the St. Johns branch of the Multnomah County Library.

16. Travel one-half block and turn right on N. Burlington Ave.

17. Travel one block and turn right on N. Willamette Blvd., taking you under the east end approach of the St. Johns Bridge.

18. As you cross Philadelphia, look to the left, toward the Willamette River, to see your first view through the bridge's Gothic arches and bents (piers on land) to the Gothic arches and bents on the other side of the river.

19. Continue another block to N. Alta Ave., turn left.

20. Travel one block and turn left on N. Edison St.

21. Crossing Philadelphia, stop under the bridge for a second and larger view of the bridge's arches and bents.

22. Continue another block and turn right on N. Pittsburgh Ave. There is a wooden sign on the corner announcing Cathedral Park.

23. Continue past Cathedral Park and the east end anchorage of the St. Johns Bridge. This massive anchorage holds the bridge's main cables, is hollow, and weighs 29,000 tons.

24. Continue one block on Pittsburgh until it dead-ends at a turnaround that has enough room for a school bus to turn. A sign reads "Welcome to the Peninsula, Gateway to Nature."

25. The floating dock in the Willamette is accessible and a good place to view Burlington Northern Santa Fe Railway Bridge 5.1, about a mile up the river, toward downtown Portland.

What to see from the dock at the St. Johns Bridge: One man who regularly fishes here advises that if you're quiet you can hear the peregrine falcons that roost on the bridge. He says, "They sound exactly like a '55 Chevy with its water pump going out." Notice the fresh water clamshells lying at the bottom of the Willamette under the gangplank leading to the floating dock. The building south of the turnaround is the Water Pollution Control Laboratory, enhanced by Don Merkt's sculpture of a water drop, and a dead-end bridge of famed landscape architect Robert Murase (1938–2005).

Next Stop: Sauvie Island Bridge
Five miles from the St. Johns Bridge

26. Backtrack on Pittsburgh, turning left on Edison.

27. Go three blocks and turn right on N. Baltimore Ave.

28. Turn right on N. Ivanhoe St. It is two blocks from here to Philadelphia and the east end of the St. Johns Bridge.

Options

At the intersection leading to the St. Johns Bridge is the St. Johns Burgerville, 8671 N. Ivanhoe St. Inside this busy restaurant hangs a large triptych (three panels, each 3x5 feet) showing the bridge as it looked when it opened in 1931. In another photograph, ironworkers eat their baloney-and-cheese sandwiches while sitting on the bridge's main cables, feet dangling high above the Willamette.

Behind the Burgerville is St. Johns Booksellers, an independent bookstore that carries this book, as well as the third edition of *The Portland Bridge Book*.

The front door faces Lombard St. (8622 N. Lombard), with store hours Sunday and Tuesday 10:00 a.m. to 6:00 p.m., and Wednesday-Saturday 10 a.m. to 8:00 p.m., tele. 503-283-0032.

29. Cross the St. Johns Bridge, staying in the right lane.

30. Turn right at the end of the actual bridge onto Bridge, the avenue.

31. Turn left onto Highway 30 toward Scappoose-St. Helens.

32. Pass through Linnton, noting the Linnton salmon, a metal sculpture on the right side of the road marking the entrance to the neighborhood. Take heed of the reduced speed limit.

33. Watch for the sign "Sauvie Island Bridge Jct. 1 mile."

34. Turn right, crossing the Sauvie Island Bridge onto Sauvie Island. The bridge, owned and maintained by Multnomah County, is located ten miles from downtown Portland.

About the Sauvie Island Bridge: The 1950 bridge, with three 200-foot-long truss spans across the Multnomah Channel of the Willamette River, is to be replaced in 2008 with a new bridge featuring a 360-foot-long tied arch span made of weathering steel. Some residents would like to see the old Sauvie Island Bridge recycled as a footbridge at NW Flanders St., across I-405 on the west side of the city. The new bridge, designed by David Evans and Associates, is the first river bridge built by Multnomah County in 50 years. It is the first river bridge in the

Portland area constructed with drilled shaft foundations. These shafts range up to ten feet in diameter and reach into the ground as much as 160 feet. For more about the new and old Sauvie Island bridges, drilled shafts, and weathering steel see pp. 101–106 and pp. 125–131 in the third edition of *The Portland Bridge Book*.

NEW SAUVIE ISLAND BRIDGE UNDER CONSTRUCTION
AT PORT OF PORTLAND TERMINAL TWO

Next Stop: Historic Hanging Deck Truss Bridge
Carrying Thurman St. Over Balch Gulch
Nine miles from the Sauvie Island Bridge

35. Follow NW Sauvie Island Rd., looping around NW Gillihan Rd. and back up onto and across the Sauvie Island Bridge to return to Highway 30. As you cross the bridge, note the huge active rock quarry somewhat to your right in the hill ahead.

36. Turn left onto Highway 30.

37. Follow the signs to the city center.

38. Angle right at the stoplight onto St. Helens Rd.

39. Follow St. Helens past Overhead Door and Shell Terminal.

40. St. Helens Rd. turns into NW Nicolai St. just past NW 31st Ave. Montgomery Park, the former home of Montgomery Ward, can be seen in the distance.

41. At the intersection of NW 29th Ave. and Nicolai, turn right onto NW Wardway, which turns into NW Vaughn St.

42. Travel uphill on Vaughn past Montgomery Park.

43. Turn right on NW 27th Ave.

44. Turn right on NW Upshur St.

45. Drive by the Old Forestry Commons sign, on your right, to the stop sign on NW 28th Ave. and Upshur. Continue on Upshur, traveling downhill.

46. At NW 29th Ave. and Upshur, choose the path toward the dead end.

47. Continue traveling uphill past residences and apartments, follow the round-about (just barely big enough for the longest school buses to turn around), and park.

48. You're in Forest Park, at the Portland Parks' Field House, headquarters for its ivy-pulling operations, 2960 NW Upshur St. There are restrooms, a water fountain, and the last of Balch Creek before it's buried for the rest of its journey to the Willamette River. Just above is the Balch Gulch Bridge and its deep truss-es hanging overhead only 25 feet above the ground.

BALCH GULCH BRIDGE HANGING DECK TRUSS

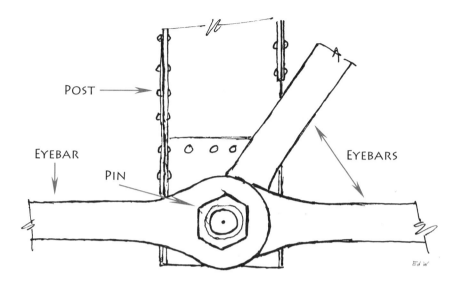

POST

EYEBAR

PIN

EYEBARS

BALCH GULCH BRIDGE'S 1905 PIN CONNECTION

About the Balch Gulch Bridge: Owned and maintained by the City of Portland, this 160-foot Pratt truss is the oldest highway deck truss in Oregon and the state's lone remaining pin-connected deck truss. It is one of only four hanging truss designs in the state. The upgrading of NW Thurman St., including the construction of this bridge, was completed in 1905 in preparation for the Lewis and Clark Exposition held nearby at Guild Lake. The structure is supported by steel trestles and overlooks Macleay Park. The stairs to the left of the bridge lead to Thurman. The bridge is scheduled for major rehabilitation by the City of Portland. For more about the Balch Gulch Bridge, see *Historic Highway Bridges of Oregon*, by Dwight Smith, et al., reprinted by the Oregon Historical Society Press, 1989.

Next Stop: The Top Deck of the Fremont Bridge
1.5 miles from the Balch Gulch Bridge

49. Backtrack on Upshur.

50. Turn right on NW 28th Ave.

51. Turn left on Thurman.

52. Follow Thurman to NW 23rd St.

53. Turn left on 23rd.

54. Turn right on Vaughn.

55. Follow signs to I-405 and the Fremont Bridge.

56. To go toward Downtown, Beaverton, and south Portland, stay right; to go toward the east side, stay in the left lanes and follow signs to The Dalles.

57. Crossing the bottom deck of the Fremont Bridge, your odometer will show you've gone 25 miles, once again proving what all bridge devotees already know: The only reason we build highways is to get from one bridge to another.

Where I Live

"Columbia River rolls big waves deep in Pacific"
The Oregonian, September 21, 2005

Two bodies of water keep a secret
like two lovers anchored
in a bathtub: rifts, drifts, abysses and ridges locked
knees to elbows under a blanket of foam
and shifting bubbles.

Each day the Columbia's plume,
"a ten-story subterranean tongue,"
forces itself into the Pacific's thermals—
union marked by whitecaps,
changing the water's skin tone,
raising temperatures.

The way I read it, a roll-a-way sky
extends a coverlet of clouds and fog,
unwraps a white terry-robed moon,
and for summer ceremonies, opens
the door of a sauna the size of the sun.

Where I live a river discharges
a hundred fifty billion gallons of fresh water
every day into blue arms—a rising
and falling from San Francisco to the Straits of Juan de Fuca.

Here, where seagulls commingle by the millions
and the shells of freshwater clams
lie scattered like tiny white pillows
under the long bed
of the St. Johns floating dock.—SWW

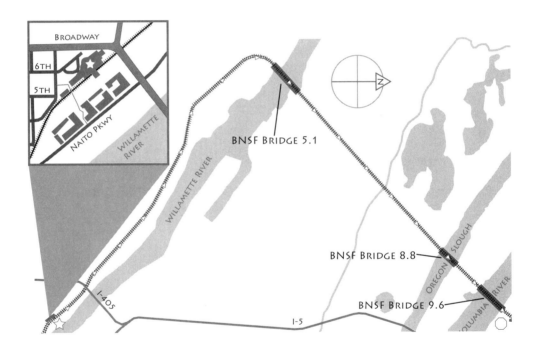

BROADWAY

6TH

5TH

NAITO PKWY

WILLAMETTE RIVER

WILLAMETTE RIVER

BNSF BRIDGE 5.1

N

I-405

I-5

OREGON SLOUGH

BNSF BRIDGE 8.8

BNSF BRIDGE 9.6

COLUMBIA RIVER

☆ START
— ROUTE
▥ RAILROAD
▷ DIRECTION
○ FINISH

Exploration Five

Amtrak from Portland, Oregon, All the Way to Vancouver, Washington Over Three Movable Bridges—And Back

This itinerary begins and ends at Portland Union Train Station.

➤ Ride for 15 minutes (9.6 miles one way) on Amtrak to Vancouver, Washington Station Depot, crossing three large movable railroad bridges.

➤ Look around Portland Station, opened in 1896. (Also see Exploration Two, "Three Bridge Central City Walk.")

➤ Visit Vancouver's historic 1908 train station and photograph or sketch the Burlington Northern Railway Bridge 9.6, located downriver (west) from the Interstate (I-5) Bridge. With a 467-foot main span, this is one of the longest swing bridges in the United States.

➤ (Optional) Visit Esther Short Park, W. Columbia St. and 8th St., in Downtown Vancouver.

Basics

Distance: 20 miles (round-trip)
Time: Two hours minimum
Fare and Timetable: See below

Portland Union Train Station
800 NW Sixth Ave.
Portland, OR 97209
503 273 4866 or 1-800-USA-RAIL

Ticketing agent available: Daily 7:30 a.m.-8:45 p.m.
Wilf's Restaurant located next door, plus a deli, newsstand, and restrooms in
the station
Wheelchair accessible

Vancouver Station Depot
1301 W. 11th St.
Vancouver, WA 98660
360 694-7308

Ticketing agent available: Daily 8:15 a.m.-8:45 p.m.
Vending machines and restrooms in the station
Wheelchair accessible

Parking in Portland: the Union Station lot, or the Smart Park at Station Place
garage, located one block north of the main station (just west of the tracks) at
the corner of NW Sixth and Lovejoy. This garage is open 24 hours, 365 days a
year, and costs six dollars a day. Portland Union Train Station is within walking
distance of the Portland Transit Mall and, after the MAX transit mall route
opens in 2009, it will be zero distance to catch a light rail train.

Smart Park at Station Place
720 NW Marshall St.
Portland, OR 97209
503-823-2885

Site Specifics

Portland Union Station is listed on the National Register of Historic Places. If you're an overnight passenger on Amtrak, there are few places with first-class waiting. The only such West Coast accommodation is Portland's Metropolitan Lounge, located just outside the doors on the east side or train side of the station. For more about Union Station, designed for the Northern Pacific Terminal Company by the architectural firm McKim, Mead, and White in 1896, go to <www.amtrakcascades.com/Portland.aspx>. For more about what to see while at the station, see Exploration Two, "Three Bridge Central City Walk."

The Northern Pacific Railroad built BNSF Railway bridges 5.1, 8.8, and 9.6 for the Spokane, Portland, and Seattle Railway Co. during Theodore Roosevelt's administration in 1908–1909. They are named for their number of miles from Portland Union Station. BNSF 5.1, across the Willamette River, was changed from a swing bridge to a vertical lift in 1989 because the 1908 bridge's clearance was insufficient for modern-day ships to pass through. For more about the Portland-area railroad bridges, see pp. 119–124 in the third edition of *The Portland Bridge Book*.

Vancouver Station Depot, opened in 1908, is an Arts and Crafts-style building that was designed with an identical front and back so station agents could serve passengers from either side. It is located at a wye, meaning it sits on a triangular patch of land with tracks on each side leading to and from BNSF 9.6, about 200 feet south. (9.6's swing span hugs the north bank of the Columbia over the main channel at river mile 106.5.) The Empire Builder, to and from Chicago, stops on the SE side of the depot, and the Coast Starlight and Cascade, to and from Seattle, stop on the west side of the depot.

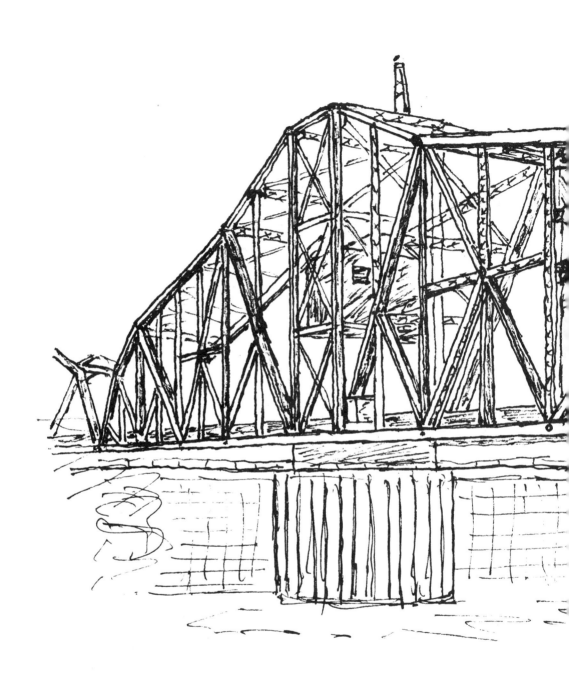

BURLINGTON NORTHERN SANTA FE RAILWAY BRIDGE 9.6
AT VANCOUVER STATION DEPOT

Option: Esther Short Park and Downtown Vancouver

Esther Short Park is six-tenths of a flat mile from the Vancouver Depot. Named for one of Vancouver's founders, the park dates to 1843. According to a sign at the entrance, it's the oldest public square in Washington state and the oldest city park in the West. It was upgraded in a $5.6 million project in 1998 that added restrooms, playground, rose gardens, a stone water fountain, and a bell tower with a glockenspiel that tells the Chinook legend of the salmon several times a day.

Directions from Vancouver Depot to the park and downtown Vancouver: Leave the depot on Hill St., walk one block; turn left (east) on W. Eighth St. and proceed five blocks to Esther St.; turn right on Esther. Many shops and restaurants are nearby.

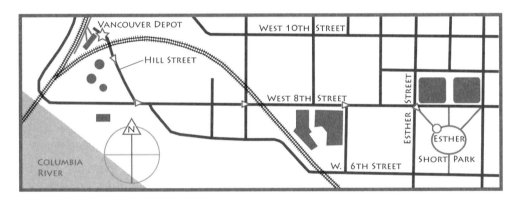

Fare and Timetable

Train Fare: $14–$22 for adults round-trip, with children (ages 2–15) half the adult fare

According to the timetable effective October 29, 2007, trains for Vancouver depart from Portland five times a day, four of them on a Talgo, a Spanish-made "bullet" train:

Cascade (Talgo)   8:45 a.m.
Cascade (Talgo)   12:15 p.m.

Cascade (Talgo)	2:50 p.m.
Empire Builder	4:45 p.m.
Cascade (Talgo)	6:15 p.m.

Trains for Portland depart from Vancouver six times a day, four of them on a Talgo:

Empire Builder	9:18 a.m.
Cascade (Talgo)	10:29 a.m.
Coast Starlight	1:08 p.m.
Cascade (Talgo)	2:19 p.m.
Cascade (Talgo)	5:19 p.m.
Cascade (Talgo)	8:29 p.m.

For example, if you leave Portland at 8:45 a.m., you arrive at Vancouver Depot at 9:00 a.m., with an hour and a half to look around before boarding the 10:29 a.m. train from Vancouver, returning to Portland at 11:00 a.m. (The schedule shows it takes longer to ride from Vancouver to Portland than it does to ride from Portland to Vancouver.)

Poem for First-Year Teachers

On Amtrak once, all the way
from Portland, Oregon
to Vancouver, Washington,

where we get off to sketch
an old riveted swing bridge,
a storyteller half a window high

informs our corner about the teacher
just retiring from the experience
of this soon-to-be-fourth grader:

At the party, she said, *Miss Hadley*
brought in pictures, pictures
of her first day teaching school
20 years ago when she wore
her black hair in long braids.

When she moved up
from second grade to third
ten years later, she started
wearing glasses.

And then there was Miss Hadley
when I met her in September.
And you know what?

You could really see it in the last picture—
It wasn't until this school year
Miss Hadley started looking like herself.—SWW

I Main Span

Soul Spans

BRIAN DOYLE

Here are some bridge stories.

Once an old man to whom I had not spoken for months, although we were neighbors, called me up in the middle of the night to help him pull in his beach stairs. Our houses were on the edge of the ocean and the ocean was furious. Out I went to meet him, in the slicing wind, and we pulled up his stairs, and I tore my hands, and shook his hand, and did not help him limp back to his house, because he was a proud and good man, as I learned later, after we met on the bridge he had made with his words.

Once I hammered a man with my fists. This was on a muddy field long ago. We punched each other until he bled and I cried with rage and exhaustion and we were pulled apart by other men. I saw him the next day in the street. We hated each other, and then he smiled. His smile was a bridge that shamed me.

Recently a friend of mine died. He was 23. I wrote a letter to his mother about his hands, which were enormous and deft. She wrote back: a small gray card, a few quiet words, her name. The card was a bridge between despair and peace.

Recently my wife was very sick. She lay in her hospital bed like a rag. She was in a pale country far from me. I kissed her with a joke in my mouth, desperate for her smile. She smiled. The leap of her lips was a bridge between lovers.

Once, long ago, when I was a small boy, I wrote a letter to my mother and left it under her plate on Mother's Day. It was a letter from Hell, refusing her admission. My father sent this letter to a small magazine, which published it and sent me a check for ten dollars. I still have that check. It is the bridge by which I became a writer.

This morning I ate breakfast with my daughter. She is an angel with an attitude, two years old. She sat in my lap and we ate raisins. Suddenly she turned and kissed me on the nose. Her kiss was made of cinnamon and milk. The brush of her breath was a bridge to my heart.

We are bound, you and I, writer and reader, by ink and paper. I sit here and tell you stories; back come your stories, sad and merry and honest. It is a curious conversation, poignant and surprising. I am moved by it. It is a gift and a lesson. It is a bridge.

Bridges Eleven

Mark Alter

Sometimes,
when the moon listens
for the nudging sun,
and after,
when the children run
confident,
catch me races,

I wonder
what the river
thinks of all its stitches,

eleven laces,

as if we,
concerned with
its exuberance,

think
it
needs mending.

Whenever I come to it

JUDITH ARCANA

I want a bridge from me to you, wherever
we are. I want to cross that bridge whenever
I come to it. I don't want the sharp speed of e-mail,
stately pace of real mail, crucial rush of FedEx
or big brown UPS. I don't want the hopeless airport
promise of security, sad grey dog of a bus
or desperate train long past the joy
of rolling overland. And I don't want any
kind of phone—voice is not enough.

But there are no bridges from me to you, no
way to come over, waving a hand, hurrying
when I see you there; no way to walk right
over the mountains, rivers; walk right over
prairies and plains. I do what I can, right
here. I walk the Steel Bridge, vibrating
with traffic, light rail, boxcars; walk Burnside's
bridge, dividing Portland, separating north
from south—useful separation, unlike ours.

I walk metal grates and slab cement on Hawthorne,
on Morrison. I consider Broadway's jumpers.
They, who must carefully weigh the deep
value of separation, want what I don't.
They break the thing I want to make.
I turn from their perch to look downriver

past the Fremont Bridge's highway ramps,
past the stolid railroad trestle, beyond those two
tough working bridges—out to distant St. Johns.

The grace of St. Johns belies its weight:
curves suggesting temples, mosques, cathedrals
where we worship the goddess of connection,
meditate on the human need for linkage.
Crowning the city's ladder of bridges,
St. Johns stretches across the need
to pull ourselves together, demonstrating
attachment, embodying our complicated struggle
to construct—and maintain—attachment.

Crossing Dark Water

ELIZABETH ARCHERS

At the place where the Broadway Bridge draws for ships
pavement becomes wooden boards;
between them, murky water sliding far below her shoes:
a moving liquid low sky transforming
the heart's eye into simple sensations,
a child's poem about sleep and the blankets and bed.
Dying becomes easy.

Light covers the river,
a rusted turquoise hull,
in gold-suffused atmospheres
at the granary unloading.
The Fremont Bridge
a pale, distant arc.
The light is fading fast.

Railing, traffic, and water
ruffled by the paddlings
of quieted ducks in their rows,
the realizations of losses and hope
converging in regret,
the vibrations underfoot,
and the breezes from cars
lift into the curve of her calves and thighs,
taking her all the way over, uphill again,
all the way home.

What You Learn
Robert Cohen

There must be some part of yourself
that you don't give away, not even for love—
a constant core, a sufficiency,
which despite all losses, you never lose.
And this center regenerates a life,
like a starfish regrowing spokes,
when you've been cut loose,
or else there would be no hope in the world,
just bridges spanning a hole
and roads to everywhere—
all connection and no soul.

Walking Across Morrison Bridge

WALT CURTIS

The Chinook wind melts
the snow. Magical is the city,
literal fairy and wizard lights,
soft as eyes. Lights soft as lips,
yet softer, luminous as
a kiss lingering on the landscape.
Gray choppy river, gray
river—I love you!
Your bridges *are* bridges—
they make connection
over something wide and deep.
The bridges of Portland
hold hands. Bridges are
the most beautiful architecture
in the world.
Cloud mists lean on black-green
West Hills like a friend
leans on a friend, on a long trip.
A cloak of mist, a cap of drops,
dressed in the December loomscape.
This city has the most
marvelous skies, dramatic
as Peking or watery volcanoes.
Backdrops of white light,
gray light, blue light,
black light. I am

an actor in the glorious
play of the windiverse.
If I was born for nothing else,
I was born to stride
across the Morrison Bridge
on this weather. I walk not
just on water, I walk on air.
I see everything, and
everything *sees* me—
in the pores of my skin,
in the gulps of my breath.

Happiness

STEPHEN DUNN

A state you must dare not enter
with hopes of staying,
quicksand in the marshes, and all

the roads leading to a castle
that doesn't exist.
But there it is, as promised,

with its perfect bridge above
the crocodiles,
and its doors forever open.

Across the River

C.A. Gilbert

There is no point believing in just one thing.
No matter how strong it is or your belief,
you will find it is connected to other things.
And these ideas may be gospel to other people
who maybe you don't agree with; can't see
yourselves being on the same team.

Our beliefs are buttresses; built slowly
to weather change the way a bridge
is designed for a river's turmoil or trestles
traverse a canyon's wicked depths.
Destinations may change, but a bridge
permits us to travel safely where
we could not go before.

Scaffolding

Seamus Heaney

Masons, when they start upon a building,
Are careful to test out the scaffolding;

Make sure that planks won't slip at busy points,
Secure all ladders, tighten bolted joints.

And yet all this comes down when the job's done
Showing off walls of sure and solid stone.

So if, my dear, there sometimes seem to be
Old bridges breaking between you and me

Never fear. We may let the scaffolds fall
Confident that we have built our wall.

The Teeth

Donna Henderson

Each time she takes her teeth out I could leap
through my skin—it's real

physical; my body, the whole body
startles at this sudden (and it's never not

sudden) undoing she does—
no warning—
so quick I can't brace for it;

casually,

the way you might pick your nose,
rub an eye—
she just

raises a hand and flips loose the whole gum load

—and loose goes a piece of what was her before,

becomes all possibility
(rows of theater seats the bleached
jaw by the water hole).

As I watch, something loosens

inside as it does driving over the Oakland-Bay
Bridge (the heart fighting to keep itself

still, the hands steadily steering)
the flesh knowing the bridge is a reach between

solids & tensions, the self
passing that way over water through ether
(strobe-like flashes of blue through the gaps
in the grating)

the span function not a ground
(composed of its solids but not
the ground)

my commute and the daily commute of my cohorts dependent
like quotidian speech
on the speed of the passage—

now the pink-&-cream guts of her smile
wave
jerk
dip in space from her fingers

while over the empties the mouth pleats now,
pinching a nothing that seemed to me solidly

something a bit ago—
as though she'd reached

down and unscrewed a live limb, all mine
tense self-assuringly, suspending their disbelief.

Breakup
DIANE HOLLAND

The river ran clear all week, just a few
rafts of ice along the edge and the dark
palette of not-yet-spring—

until something broke loose far upstream,
filling the river with angular slabs of ice,
a tumbling clamor, jostling, churning,
a crystalline city come undone,
roaring downriver with dull thumps, sharp
cracks like shots fired, jagged floes piling up
while a whirlpool of smaller shards traps
what can't resist.

I'm caught on what now seems a frail bridge,
feel each shudder as ice rams the supports,
sets the whole structure atremble—
I'm dizzy with what rushes toward me,
what streams away, until I'm the
one still point.

And I suddenly hear my mother's last words
before her final silence—
I am a skyscraper turned on its point,
all the doors and windows open, everything
is falling out. Me too, I thought then,
I must be among that rubble, left behind,

a soul-shudder I wasn't braced to allow.
Within the huge chunks of ice, I see a lifeline
locked in place—sapphire of the deepest past,
pressed clear as glass, layers of crystal lattice,
purest white laced with darker bands
where winds drifted the summer dust.
This is old ice.

Maybe this is what it will be like, at the end,
to let go, be taken up by the maelstrom,
tumbled back to elemental grit and water.
There will come this torrent
and no place to stand.

The Bridge
LAWSON INADA

of my nose
is constructed
to cross:

Hello.

Dishwater

TED KOOSER

Slap of the screen door, flat knock
of my grandmother's boxy black shoes
on the wooden stoop, the hush and sweep
of her knob-kneed, cotton-aproned stride
out to the edge and then, toed in
with a furious twist and heave,
a bridge that leaps from her hot red hands
and hangs there shining for fifty years
over the mystified chickens,
over the swaying nettles, the ragweed,
the clay slope down to the creek,
over the redwing blackbirds in the tops
of the willows, a glorious rainbow
with an empty dishpan swinging at one end.

Around the World

SARAH LANTZ

An hour or so before dawn
a mother startles from a bird's cry
which she hears as her child's waking.
Breathless, she finds the child sound asleep.
The well-taught mother mutters to herself
how stupid and climbs back
under the covers relieved

as a different mother
taught less well, steadies
herself with the flush
of her child's face, which
she worries but never reveals
is too radiant to be her relation,
and wandering back to bed
wonders if it was the sound
of her own waking she heard,

as still another mother
asleep next to her child
holds her breath
and waits motionless, listening
until the bird cries again
and her alarm has a name,
a change of tune outside
like a first hint of smoke,

and shivers run through her
like all mothers when
there is nowhere to run
no way to go forward or backward
and in her arms the only bridge.

Demographic

DORIANNE LAUX

It's time for me to walk to the bus stop
and sit down among them, the man
tied into his wheelchair, the woman
with the humped back, time for me
to kneel and hold his cup while he adjusts
his books and his pack, look up at her
flowered blouse, his scratched glasses.
There's a sky full of rain that won't
come down, pigeons asleep on the lawn,
and across the street pumpkins piled high
in front of the market, Xeroxed flyers
stapled to the telephone pole. To the east
a day moon above the bridge, cars
filing under like a school of fish,
and if I watch my feet, I won't knock over
the plastic dish the blind man has filled
to the brim for his dog. It's time
to go to work, to wait while they gather
their belongings, while the metal mesh
platform unhinges and bangs down,
time to nod to the driver as he pulls
back on the lever and a man lifts
into the air, to cup her elbow, thin wing,
to enter the threshold and stand
among them, listen to their murmurs,
the news of the day, to slip my hand through
the frayed canvas noose and hold on.

Bridgekeeper

MELISSA MADENSKI

Riding the mustard yellow
Broadway bus, just a child
thin enough to bounce
on brown cracked leather
seats. Wheels
echo
over scrolled patterns of iron and air,
over the bridge's center grid,
over metal skids,
shudder
where gates rise up
for the big ships.

I imagine myself
the bridgekeeper high
above the ribbon of river
in a room balanced
on steel beams,
a room with one candle
on an Asian plate, with books,
lots of books,
a room with charts
hung, corners folding up
from below,
a room with one light
under a soft brown shade,
a beacon to guide
me and the big ships
to safe harbor.

Blinking

MORTON MARCUS

You've got to love life so much that you don't want to miss a moment of it, and pay such close attention to whatever you're doing that each time you blink you can hear your eyelashes applauding what you've just seen.

In each eye there are more than 80 eyelashes, forty above and forty below, like forty pairs of arms working, 80 pairs in both eyes, a whole audience clapping so loud you can hardly bear to listen.

160 hands batter each other every time you blink. "Bravo!" they call. "Encore! Encore!"

Paralyzed in a hospital bed, or watching the cold rain from under a bridge—remember this.

White Birds

JOY MCDOWELL

I sensed you watching the egrets from your bed, counting
their spindle-legged number. Every afternoon I sat on that
stranded log below your house, a log that reminded me of a
ship's bridge, the place where the captain gives the orders.
Even a fictional starship has a bridge. I gripped the broken
limbs of that bleached giant and imagined I was in charge
of the whole blasted universe. And I gave the orders. You
were not supposed to die, not yet, not at the age of fifty.
Only the egrets were there to listen. Perhaps they carried
my whispered demands high into the sky before releasing
them into the wind.

Ice Storm Paralyzes City

Michael McDowell

Poets hope for extremes in weather—
It's part of the job.
Sure, sure, antennae of the race,
Speaking the eternal verities,
Poets yearn for spring,

But spring comes too soon and too easily.
Daffodils now in February,
And Portland still hasn't had a big snow,
A big freeze and silver thaw.
We haven't yet known we're alive

By seeing the world's heart stop:
The crack and whoosh of a fallen branch
Too loaded with ice to hold,
The rifle shot cry of wood too cold
To stay silent—

We hope for the brittle hard world of legendary winter
To stop commerce and the quotidian
And in the deathly tranquil city to tell us:
Look at your breath: You, are, alive.
Look at how little you need to survive.

Mathematics, Movement & Arugula
Sid Miller

I.
By the bourbon on her breath
you will understand equations mathematical,
those involving variables, no value
ever constant, no number
itself. By the black bra slung
over the back of the dining room chair
you will return, deny the logic
of calculus, rely on that of the salivary
glands, the far-off scent of a charring
porterhouse. Sometime between
the collapse of sleep and divisor of day,
you might wake from your own restlessness,
use the inexact angle of shadows
to render the sweat from her skin
and coax the air back down.

II.
Today you walk the bridges of Portland:
Steel, Burnside, Morrison and Hawthorne,
east on one, west on another. Naturally
there is a drizzle and a point in the afternoon
when you want to stop,
rest, but unnaturally—you don't.
You walk the tightrope of separation,
find the Willamette below moves at one speed,

traffic at another, thoughts at one
totally distinct—without the crutch
of linear movement. By the time you return
to your car you are more than damp
from perspiration, your feet sore, your ideas
of motion awash. When the engine turns over
you don't require more thought, home inevitable,
the route etched in the pavement.

III.
Dirt stains on the knees of your jeans
serve as indication, but the ritual dressed
in slippers that glide across the carpet
offer little else. You stand, the coffee's
steam fogs the sliding glass door.
Beyond, the arugula is flower,
the tomatoes have split, the roots of the green
onions—the size of cipollinis, the bed,
this other kind, the one that nearly broke you—
has filled in with weed—criminals,
or more accurately, con men.

IV.
You were taught to never go anywhere
without nouns. That abstraction is a blind man
in the desert. You make a list: long legs,
oysters, jungle gym, lipstick, on and on,
each image to evoke memory, each one
to be slowly crossed off. There's

a headache comes from the weight
of concrete. You let it, put your head
down on your arms, let the woman next to you
nudge you back up. But already
it's too late, it has started; you afloat,
on some nondescript wave of theory (love,
hate, etc.), nowhere and everywhere simultaneously.
For our sake you begin to drool,
for yours, we let you alone,
to float on, to the infinite,
or some other such unallowed place.

Bridge
ADA MOLINOFF

For Rabbi Emeritus Joshua Stampfer
Congregation Neveh Shalom
Portland, Oregon

His voice wafts from the library
into my hurrying. I seek the empty chair,
notice the table has been burnished
by the arms of many learners.
The man next to me opens
the Mishnah to an ancient passage,
points out the place.

"The sacrifice of goats must halt—
wood offerings are prohibited."
That community was under siege.
Supplies were scarce, or gone.
Sacred obligations
could not be met.

Rabbi dwells on the story, helps us to hear
the anguish when a holy rite ceases.
We touch the Hebrew phrases;
our fingers travel the page,
trace with him a bridge
between our forebears
and this room.

Detour

ERIK MULLER

The bridge is out: I must
drive away from where I want to go,
double back three times as far.
There are strange houses on the ridges
with views toward the places I know.
People standing beside mailboxes are surprised
to see me. They pause before turning back indoors.
There are roads whose curves bring walls
of leaves right to my face. Have these people
always lived here? Have there always been
such steep views of town?
If I stop the car now and get out,
if I speak to anyone here, I will never
finish the life I am living.
Could my tongue be at home in another language?
How could I ever win another wife?
Or at childbirth be an enthusiastic father?
What could I say at the new deaths
that seemed so much like the old?
If I thought about my neighbors here
I would become sad since I never spoke to those others.
Perhaps I would receive letters about gardens and cats.
I must drive on. I rely on
the chance to return to where I began.
Hope for the bridge to open soon.

City of Bridges

ERIN OCON

Vyctoria wonders what's over there,
her child's eyes wide, as she gazes
at the sloping Thurman Street Bridge.

I say "Nothing" too quickly, turn off for the park.
But as we tromp through damp morning grass,
and stain our hands with blackberries, the bridge
still looms above us. Vyctoria stares, pleads
to go up when we're done. I tell her it's just
some houses on a hill, but finally agree.
Over the bridge, the homes spring up and she states
the obvious: they're big. I quickly U-turn, and we
coast back down, pretending it's been fun.

It's only a few miles back to her house, but it
requires another bridge crossing. She falls silent,
gazes down at the river, glimpses cranes building
condos that line the remaining west side.
We're driving east.

I exit at Killingsworth, continue past the discount
shops, the bus stop. The sun begins to break
through the clouds, shining on the dark skin of
the young men waiting. Skin that matches her own.
We arrive at her yard, browning with summer;

she climbs over a chain-link fence, knocks on
the door of the crouching ranch home.
I drive west again, to my place across the river.
The skin in the streets begins to match my own.

Sometimes I think city bridges are ill named.
Serving less to connect, and more to
remind of the space still between.

The Briefest Bridge
SUSAN PARKER

The briefest bridge
spans life to none
In a breath
you cross
and we are left
afraid to follow
where you are not waving

Lane Change
PAULANN PETERSEN

A snapshot glance over my shoulder,
and I make my move, quick, thinking
how easy, how simple to
not see, to hit, be hit: the blindside
slash of metal, of glass,
my flesh driven back into the sharp
of my own teeth and bones.
Smashed just like that,
and maybe not even a stop

for pain. Maybe my mind
plucks me away from my done-for
body, lets me think I live on,
still driving the now gone-to-scrap car
onto the arc of bridge that each day routes me
home. Driving up, over the river's sheen,
cresting above midflow, then down
onto the other side and off, until it's all
a pure coast.

Maybe my mother's last years
were such a thing. Those motionless,
voiceless days not days or nights
at all, not a senseless dragging
of flesh, not some nightmare sleep
that kept her awake enough

to chew, to swallow,
her bowels and bladder emptied
by tubes. Not that, but just
her behind the wheel,
some sun easing through the windshield,
dust whispering along the dash,
a tune she likes on the radio,
little hum harboring somewhere
in her throat. Here comes the approach
to the bridge, and another driver stops
long enough to let her into the line
of crossing cars. A wave of thanks,
then a slow climb to the part
she likes best, at the bridge's crest.
There she can glimpse a mountain's point
and a river's mirror length,
the part that could just as well last forever
if anyone bothered to ask her.
Up and over the narrow span—that one drive
she could do in her sleep,
the easy one, home.

Beginning to Find Your Way

RITA OTT RAMSTAD

What do you do when the bridge to your future
begins sinking into the sand of your life,
the footings disappearing into the vast beach
of all you've done wrong?

That span of steel and concrete seemed immovable,
solid as your surest convictions,
but now that you are on it, you can feel
it listing, and you don't know what to do.

Should you run across it lightly,
carrying nothing but your hope
to make it to the other side before the whole thing goes under?

Should you creep your way back
to some solid ground, see if you can somehow start
over, find a whole new bridge to a whole different place?

But what of those who have come across with you?
What if they refuse to run forward or turn back, insist
on making their slow way across this structure that you fear
cannot hold, will not even acknowledge the waves
beginning to splash over its railing and onto your feet?

Perhaps there is another way.
Perhaps it is not over the waters of your life, but into them:

Perhaps you need to hold the hands of those you love and dive
with faith, leave the idea of bridges in your past, plunge
into the dark green waters that have always seemed
too cold, too deep, too murky for the likes of you.

Yes, if you had jumped when the bridge still towered above
them, those waters would have met your body
like pavement greeting a suicide from the 32nd floor.

But look, the bridge has fallen so low
that all you have to do now is slip into them.

See how, from this distance, the water is more clear than green.

Feel how, when you dip your leg in and leave it there,
your skin adjusts to its temperature,
begins to find its way to something like warmth.

Hear how, when the waves lap the shore of the islands
that have suddenly risen all around you, each a different place
you might land, they murmur like your mother's voice did
all those years she soothed away your fears.

Eight Ways of Looking at a Bridge

Carlos Reyes

> *For Jorge Carrera Andrade*

I.

Bridge over dying waters,
you arch like a bow and ready
your arrows to shoot at passing clouds
to bring pure rains back to the river.

II.

Aeolian harp, your taut wires
played by whichever wind
that runs the canyons you watch over.

III.

Instrument itself, holes through
your girders whistle a song
that sends pigeons flying.

IV.

The falcon owns the bridges,
nests in its struts
knows the moan
is not song, but

the liquid coo
of pigeons strutting
about to meet death
in his talons.

V.

Night's great drama
the full moon sliced
as it rises through
suspension cables.

But like the woman
sawn in half, this magician's
moon is whole again
once above the arching span.

VI.

. . . A butterfly suture,
that holds together flesh
on either side of
a great flowing wound.

VII.

The moon looks down
on the dark skeletal bridge . . .

VIII.

Crossing cars, trucks, bicycles
see none of this, the airplane
has a better chance of viewing
the span, but sees only
an ink line cutting a river
into silver segments.

The plane needs but the arcing air
to cross seas to other continents,
following the curvature of the earth.
Its great circle route, the longest bridge.

Walking Home from Work During the Last Week of Our Marriage

KIRSTEN RIAN

You are home by now,
probably even have tea made,

coat's on the bed, the day
you left behind drifting,

you thumb through the mail,
refill the cat's food, water,

I wind the neighborhood blocks
around the maypole of our house,

unable to turn up our driveway,
so I continue on down other people's streets

glancing in windows where the light is on,
harvesting stars by looking up

and saving the sight of millions
of dangling lights bigger than they seem

for days that could be better.
I walk past a yard strewn

with balls, a tricycle, watering cans,
and where the grass stops the sidewalk

continues the symphony of play
with chalk drawings spilling

off the curb and into the street,
UFOs, space men, flowers, dragons,

and a purple bridge arching across
the expanse of the still, dark street,

awaiting morning's rain
to blur the dust that drew them.

Piercing One Ear

WILLA SCHNEBERG

That self-important Portland *momzer*,
the nose and throat man
with the laquerware Chinese urns.
Where does he think he is, on Park Avenue?
He thought he could show up
the New York doctors
and make me dine again. At Bishop Morris,
I, too, would hold a glass of water
to my lips and swallow
just like the other *alte kakers*.

He sent me for a CAT Scan
and got my hopes up,

but the bridge between the pharynx
and my gullet has been blown up.
No Army Corps of Engineers
will come to the rescue.
Food can't leap from one side
to the other. Perhaps Dr. Botox
thought he could string a hammock.

I was always a sucker
for suspension bridges—
how their sides raise up to the sky
and seamlessly remerge.

For my consolation prize
the great man repierced my left ear.
It closed up from all the aggravation.
I appreciate symmetry. With two holes
I can wear earrings again.
Tomorrow I'll model
the blue-green stone ones
my daughter brought from Jerusalem.

Note to the reader: *momzer* is Yiddish for bastard and *alte kakers*
is a Yiddish expression meaning something like "old farts."

Traffic Jam on the Ross Island Bridge

Peter Sears

For Dennis Meiners

No car backlights move. I am knuckled in here
on the Ross Island Bridge at 5:17 p.m., heading west,
against rush-hour traffic, toward the West Hills
of Portland. The hills are ridged by trees in silhouette
against the sunset. Strands of clouds loll over the trees,
sink into them, and snag. One strand settles in the trees
like a big, gray nest. If there is no Northwest bird
that lays its eggs in such a nest, inventing it is my job.
My potter friend and I will envision the bird
of weightless nests. I will tell my friend that white
sunset comes down on the nest and shimmers it;
and darkness, thick with rain, pushes the light down
into the trees. There is not enough sky for the rain
below it. Why hurry? This is Oregon, rain is lazy here.
Wind shoots the rain up in sheets that topple back
through themselves. Between the treeline and
the darkness falling over the line are planes of light,
measuring miles across. Rain does not faze them.
These slabs of light slide through themselves,
nimble triangles, across the entire city. I'd love
to have one slab hover over my backyard some
early evening, and take my friends out to toast it.

Autumn

JOSEPH A. SOLDATI

Last night a vintage trolley
almost collides with the full moon
Tangled in the web of the old Steel Bridge.
In a shower of sparks it stopped,
waited for the moon to roll down the silver tracks
before it gathered speed and bounced
into the darkening sky above the West Hills.

Today the morning gleams gold, almost cold,
and as clear as crystal quartz;
the wind flails redyellowbrown leaves
off the trees, scatters them like cowards
in a mob, and flings them into oblivion.
Belligerent even to buildings,
it loosens siding from sides
with a thin aluminum rattle.

The pier's pilings wear cocked hats
of cormorants airing their wings,
Thick round derbies of gulls,
and one old stovepipe of a heron,
hunkered down so it won't blow off
into the wind-roughed river
where chandeliers of sunlight
gleam beneath the surface,
lighting the way for salmon and steelhead
on their way upstream to spawn and die.

Notes on St. Johns Bridge (an excerpt)
DOUG SPANGLE

This is the way
        to cross the water:
                a section of arc,
trajectory for thought to travel on; participation,
vault, arch, synaptic glidepath,
           cables iron vines garlanding
the blue spaces of separation
        between North and South.

Ahead of me, through iron archways,
        St. Helens' equilateral wreathes smoke like a censer,
        Adams a vague emblem in obscurity,
        Rainier a diadem so distant it's almost not there,
        Hood a white wing stretched out over the city;
All waiting for sunset, all fading slowly away;

St. Johns' spires
        aspire into blue,
           bugle

up
  ascend ascend
      this way;

      from shale to ivy;
      from ivy to hawthorn;
      flesh to brown to green to blue.

Amazing that steel could be so much a reverence:
Structure so real so adequate,
        a necessity in the landscape.

By Hawthorne Bridge
WILLIAM STAFFORD

They went on talking about the river.
They stopped sometimes, then began
again, faster, picking up what they had
said before and moving it along. Their
voices made me remember a time
on a train, people in another compartment
traveling home and telling about it while
we dozed. And we woke up at dawn all turned
around, passing trees in a line with their tops
just above mist that swirled around us.
The world was all gray, and we shivered while we moved.

The Song of the Bridge

DAVID STEINMAN

With hammer-clang on steel and rock
  I sing the song of men who build.
With strength-defying storm and shock
  I sing a hymn of dreams fulfilled.

I lift my span, I fling it wide,
  And stand where wind and wave contend.
I bear the load so men may ride
  Wither they will, and to what end.

The light gleams on my strands and bars
  In glory when the sun goes down.
I spread a net to hold the stars
  And wear the sunset as my crown.

Birds, Probably Birds

DIANNE STEPP

Waking this morning I thought of her,
and tonight walking the deck to see the stars.
I'd see her driving past with groceries,
or last spring setting out daisies
in her newly spaded bed.

I thought of her lying in the river
not far from here, under the bridge.
The milky explosion when she landed,
the unbelievable silt.
And of the one who held her in his arms,
the trees bending down,
the freshness of the air there
above the earth's lung.

Birds, probably birds that morning,
as always, and probably the scent
on her skin, in her hair, her limp body
pressed against his chest, recalled the briefest
moment of tenderness, a twitch
at the corner of his eye, before he dropped her
into the river from the bridge,
believing she would never be found.

Town Is a Lamp in the Window

SANDRA STONE

we drive by all our lives,
an illuminated flash, that recurs and subsides,
an almost-face that looks out
on the drizzled street,
the crazed grays of a glass
that mirrors winter.

Town is the imprimatur that calls us home,
that tranced outpost
imprinted
on the mind's first primer,
a luminous toy yard,

a single tree with dropsical fruit,
a cup of shadows that tipsily fall across the slate,
the enthralled alphabet of beasts
on the frieze of the easel,
the handkerchief rabbit on the yawning wall.

The first town is within us,
houses like ports that pulsate with light,
undulant evening that falls
dazed to the feat of the calendar,
the imagined kitchen with its rustic bouquet,

confetti linoleum, superior for polka
when the child bobbed
on the father's uplifted shoes,
and shadow, behind.
Now, the tiny door to the cellar

gives way to the collapsible staircase.
Now, objects in milky shrouds,
ghosts of the laundry
mold in their archaic graves.
That is the topography we revert to,
mind—memory's preserve

that bridges the curtained
outpost
we view from a passing window,
fleet and dim,
as from an auto,
amazed,

the little parents in a district
that no more exists—
indistinct luminous lamp-lit
hometown
by whatever name it persists.

Reckoning

Colette Tennant

My body was circled by the moon's whiteness
Night was a sonata.
White was the moon's
only adopted child.
Every blade of grass
ached with an epic
heard by fireflies and wind.
The moon covers my eyes
with shadows: am I
being forgotten?
Oh, my lovely years—
they knew how to cross the river
without a bridge.
The Big Dipper and Little Dipper know each other.
Between them my mouth opens
and I taste earth.
Many days I watched white-faced clouds
chase my kite toward the sun.
My red boots were licorice
feeding the sidewalk.
I was alone once
locked in red velvet,
a secret.
I still see her sometimes
in early evening.
Now she stands on a limestone cliff

looking for a song
she thought was a hymn.
I walk,
one hand under the trees,
the other in the rain.
The moon is a singer, too,
her memory
as long as the shore.

Natural Bridge

Jack Turteltaub

I would choose bridge
—if I could be one thing—
like this soaring buttress of stone
with its vista
of rock, sage and sky,
a stunning purity.
This span spreads its torso
over a rough but sensuous space,
conceals crevices and coves
in which insects settle
and animals browse
in the morning's dewy chill
or in the freshening breeze
of a slick-rock evening.
This bridge also hides,
under its backbone,
below its vertical conceits,
water singing and tumbling
—in invisible currents—
because it's humble sand and clay,
stones tumbled for centuries
deposited in a small, parched gully
embroidered by Russian olive,
desert rose, canyon oak,
a juniper or two,
leaves entwined in a promise
that spurs my wish to know

the epochs of stasis and motion:
water's constant flow.
Once, these molecules shifted, rolled:
soil was carried far in floods
and with extreme violence
by the polarity in itself,
so that, purified,
the granules could settle by aggregation,
the slow accretion of gravity
in sequences of deposition and exposition
—and water, wind could sculpt again
what eons had begun,
that which earth had elevated,
carving these new forms:
monoliths, pinnacles and cliffs
more fragile than they looked,
curvaceous monuments
to exertions of magnetism and gravity
to the shape shift of land forms,
the scrape of lizard and tumbleweed
sand particles loosening
from scalloped scarps,
the impenetrable silences:
time quoting itself.
Impossible, I know, but
I wish I could flow,
tumble and pound like a river,
settle, compress,
solidify into seabed
then rise as this creamy arch of stone

—like a conjurer's astounding trick—
yet for a few millennia
be strong enough to uphold
the beauty in apparent solidity.
In this shifting prospect,
be a path to proceed:
ark, art and apogee.

Sentence Span
Victoria Fairham Wheeler

A sentence spans a page

    like a   road 'cross a vast midwestern county

But oh, the corners to turn

    That's where adventure lies

Writers spit landmarks out the window in the wind.

The curious hitchhike along behind

At rest stops they idle

ponder road conditions

anticipate the next town

    snap a photo

        of the bridge.

Blue Heron

Victoria Wyttenberg

She is the blue distance
of everything we kiss,
the guttural cry of departure.
How can any of us protect ourselves?
My husband turns from me
and the dead slip in.
The heron is bent
like an old woman.
She is a solitary feeder
and I am afraid
my very presence drives her away,
but I return often
when she isn't there,
watching changes of light
on water. I look for blue
on the edge, the promise
of plumage. When I least
expect it, the heron appears,
still as wood pilings.
She knows how to avoid
storms and how to be alone,
staying in shallow margins,
waiting. The air is cold
as earth. My body is turning blue.

Weather Poem

SOPHIE ZAFFINA

A divining rod floats pointing north.
From a bridge I can lean down
to a refrigerator borne almost upright,
a narrow dock ferrying a gull.
Green-bumpered tugboats barrel
downriver, corral the lost.
I follow the branch's wake south to another
bridge where a friend I last saw in 1990
surfaces, heroin and two suicide attempts
clinging to his cropped blond head.
He knows me before I know him.
He was near death in a field once.
The flood has risen him back
to a night of rain blurring the concrete,
how he introduced me
to Wagner, the Balinese gamelan, Tibetan
monks chanting through pipes as long as a river,
voices growling from the deep
of the deepest.

11 Beyond Local Piers

The Whisperer

MARY BARNARD

Where the sea runs a cobalt wedge under the coast bridges
and rhododendrons burn cool above concrete piers, an eddy of air
at the bridgehead will be I, as much I as
walks alone here between watered lawns at moonrise.

The eyes lie in daytime, that say these chairs, fields,
faces, are I, who am a strand of air traveling in the sound of leaves.
If the winds of the soul be unconsumed, I am lost,
left clinging at a bridgehead over sea water.

There is no reprieve in the touch of flowering trees.
Finger is sister to bark, both mute and solid, both
independent in death. Pity the poor soul, the public wind
imaged in language, proud to whirl papers down a littered street,
a draft at the door, whining for the bellows under your ribs.

Where We Stand

JONAH BORNSTEIN

I want to take you with me,
erase the fractures of time and tend
again a garden planted with seeds
of unknown origin, to wait
for summer, when we unearth
the shy roots of harmony.

I cannot shed the weapons
I have wrought, cannot clip
the limbs that balance
me—but I can be a brace
against the rapids that plunge
around you, I can be a bridge

for you to walk across; look down
into the river and you will see
the patterns of trees, the shadows
of leaves, the form of my love for you.

Do not fold yourself
into the crib of ice cast
in the rocks at the headwaters;
it holds nothing but sorrow,
frozen at the edge of our lives.

I want to rise from the base
of the gorge, extend up to you,
your reflection rippling
on the surface, because I love you
and I am drawing enough water
to hold us both a long time.

Synchronous Vertical Excitation
JOSEPHINE BRIDGES

With a nod to Portland Parks' Poetry & Bridge Walks

The difference
between me
and Howard Crombie
is that every time he
walked across
the narrow arch
of stone and sod
that the sea far below
had spent centuries carving
out of Cape Arago, he
jumped up and down
three times
as hard as he could,
tempting fate, whereas I
leaped lightly just once,
because he was watching,
and would have tormented me
otherwise.

Not long after
my one and only
ill-advised, pathetic
suicide attempt,

the sea took back
its bridge, but neither
Howard Crombie nor I
were anywhere near
at the time.

Celilo Fishermen
ED EDMO

you made your nets
& tested the knots
    seeing that they held.

little did you know
    what was to hold you
    after the sound of
    water falling
    over what
        used to be.

Walkway

JEAN ESTEVE

Who does not stop
when crossing the bridge
over Alsea Bay
stop and look over
the delicate rail
to barnacled stones
old and patient
lying below.

Of those who stop
stop and gaze down
at long-weathered stones
who does not spit
then watch the lacy
delicate pellet
float toward the cold
gray water.

Of those who spit
over filigree breastwork
then let their gaze
follow its drift
who does not think
of themselves dressed in lace
winsome and delicate
hurtling downward.

Beside Alsea Bay Bridge
RUTH HARRISON

if you are watching light
  late in a summer of little wind
    Where do you rest, oh wings?
      beyond bridge understructure
        estuary water gleams silken
          in afternoon's uncolored light
            swallows dart and swoop
              beside Alsea Bay Bridge
            among a thousand midges
          above that silver reflection
        black movements interlace
      spanning earth, sky, earth
    You've made homes under this traffic?
  from a certain angle, you see
slants of concrete, arabesques of flight

Manhattan Red

DAVID JOHNSON

A railway bridge spanning
the 300-foot Crooked River Gorge
once bore a signature
in crimson letters two feet high:

MANHATTAN RED

Who was this traveler from the Big Apple
who left his jaunty autograph on the High Lonesome?
A bindlestiff riding the rails with legs dangling?
A stewbum heading toward warmer days in California?
I can imagine Red nabbing a gallon of paint and a brush
from a construction site in Madras or Redmond,
holding on fist-tight to the iron girder
while he leaned over the river to slather
his moniker on the rusty, auburn siding.
I can hear him now, telling his whiskery yarns
while coyotes howl around the campfire.

One Morning

KATY MCKINNEY

You will wake before dawn,
slip into your car,
and leave your mountain home
while the stars are still out.

So early you share the road
only with log trucks,
you will travel downhill
all the way to the Columbia
to cross the bridge at Hood River.

At the tollbooth
when you hold out coin or ticket,
the tollbooth operator will shake his head,
beckon you close, look both ways.
"There's a new rule," he will say, eyes on your face.
"When you cross the river in the hour before dawn,
when the hillside town is still asleep,
when there are no other cars on the bridge behind you
and only one barge cruising beneath;
when the sky is not blue, but gold and pink
above the rocky, forested walls of the gorge;
when these colors and mountains perfectly reflect
on a river so still it hasn't yet dreamt
of the colorful sails that will leap and fly
through this afternoon's wind pouring in from the east . . ."

He will pause, again looking both ways.
"It's free," he will whisper, waving you on. "It's free."

Connections at Bear Wallow Creek
DAVID MEMMOTT

Two spiders spin
over shimmering water
with limbs of soft down.

The ceremony
of Spring's vibrating wings
resolves in midair.

Spiders may not appreciate
the music they make—
only tension in lines

alerts them to light's
connections swinging
through trees.

Their tapestry tremors with dew
and windblown thistledown dismembers
their living bodies of web.

Without these thin lines
seasons do not connect,
stars drift, and the moon

falls into the sun.

On the Willamette Bridge—17 June '05

Margaret Gish Miller

It's not that the man was alone,
a rope tied around
his neck. In the gridlock,

a few feverish motorists
called out to him,
Jump, Asshole, while other drivers

ran out of gas. Some held
their cell phones
like anchors.

One motorist, marooned,
turned to music, to Muddy Waters,
whose voice swam like silk

across the Willamette, a place
where Natives once floated
like salmon, no bridge of cars above.

Beneath the bridge, lost
souls are living in makeshift
homes. And in another

car, a couple headed for
Spirit Mountain sat still,
a bottle of whiskey between

them. Some starlings flew
above. Some boys peered out
and saw a man on the bridge with a rope.

Lament

AMY KLAUKE MINATO

The woman walks to a footbridge
that sways like a spider's line
above Desolation Creek
and lies down.

Clouds whorl the sky
like her infant's hair
when she cradled him
on her lap, still
as a peach. Below her
the stream keens and roils

while salmon lay eggs
on gravel beds in the slow
currents along the shore
and then turn over
onto the glass plate of the water
to die. This

is how it should be
parents gone first
the young poised
and gleaming into their lives.

Not these stammering hands
these swollen breasts

spilling milk. A kick
shuddered her belly
then nothing. The bridge rocks
as wind rises. Above her geese pulse
dark veins across the sky.

At the Metolius River, We Walk in Falling Snow

Judith Montgomery

We step together from the porch
into late winter's violetting dark.

About us, February flurries its snow
smatter, veil looping blued drifts

piled against the bridge-rail. Freezing waters
flex below to an avalanche of falls.

We fall silent in the river's hush. Stand
isolated, chill, in the brilliant hush of snow.

*

Once, these woods summered us in green.
Now alder's frost-bowed, weighted under white.

The lone dipper exercises joint by stiff joint,
bobbing on a black rock compromised in ice.

Overhead, in perilous geometry,
Ponderosas plunge to a frozen halt.

Snags seared by lightning thrust snow-blind.
Mauls of wind crack everything apart.

You move away, to crumbling river's-edge.
I shiver on a ledge of cold.

*

But then, above, across the shut sky,
paired geese wing and cry—*here, home.*

You turn, we turn to each other through the dark,
while snow shadows land, water, rock

to essential bones: each tree its ladder, bird
its scarf of song. Each branch its load of beauty.

Our hands a bridge to cross the coming night.

Ode to Mackinac

CHARLIE WHITE

Where the strait water flows
From Michigan to Huron
lies a small village.
Those who live there
pronounce it MAC in aw.
Furs were ferried there
in mackinaw boats;
the *couriers de bois,* who ferried the furs,
wore mackinaw jackets.
And at night, everyone slept under
mackinaw blankets.
After enlarging our language,
the villagers crafted a bridge.
All who see Big Mac are awed
by its tower and cable vernacular,
by the way the armor-plated piers
reject ice no matter how stiff winter's kiss.

Note to the reader: Mackinac and Mackinaw have the same
pronunciation. Mackinaw was the principal inland post for the
fur trade in the eighteenth century. Mackinaw was originally a
French trading post for *couriers de bois,* the fur traders.

On the Stone Bridge at Multnomah Falls

DOREEN GANDY WILEY

    Standing on the stone bridge
I follow the irrevocable fall
of the water. "Five hundred
and forty-two feet is something greater
than man," I shout, but words spin
away, plunge down tangible path
of the falls, through space, leading
to eventual kilowatts somewhere, but here

       only

          the fall

             of the water.

    Small gray water bird dips
for insects in the spray. Chance moves
as thinly as these insect wings—one
move off course and flight patterns veer,
changed forever.

    Sun cools around red cedar,
purple foxglove, rocks stained green,
thick as paint from a palette knife.

In this deaf scene only one voice
is heard. Water is the artist.

Through fjords of foliage, layers
of mist, thin as glass, only
the irrevocable fall of the water.

III Distant Approaches

Two Bridges

ELEANOR BERRY

In length and design, they had nothing
remarkable about them, though one
was notorious among drivers. Modest spans,
they carried their roadways across
ordinary obstacles—tracks for commuter
trains to New York, the second-largest river
in Connecticut, far behind the one that gave
the state its name. But for me, growing up
only child of parents who never took a trip
beyond the couple hours' drive
to my grandmother's house, these two,
between them, defined the range
of bridges.

        One I had to brave
twice each schoolday, on my walk
from home and back. I'd pass fearlessly by
the yard where a pair of boxer dogs
leapt, fiercely barking, at the fence,
but as I neared the bridge, I'd dawdle
if any cars were starting across it, hurry
if there were none. Narrow two-lane,
built of heavy timbers, it bottlenecked
Courtland Avenue above the New York,
New Haven, and Hartford line. I'd aim
to speed-walk its entire length
during a break in the traffic, not to get caught

on the walkway while a car was driving,
ka-thunk-a-thunk, ka-thunk-a-thunk,
down the plank deck beside me—or, worse,
while two squeezed by in opposite directions,
rattling every board, or a train underneath
shuddered the whole structure.

                        The other
I awaited and savored, leaning forward
from the back seat of my parents' Buick on every
rare drive up the Merritt Parkway
to my grandmother's in Meriden. This bridge
was high—seemed high to me, perched,
short-legged, on the slick edge of the leather seat—
and the water below seemed wide. What I loved
about the four-lane span that stretched
over that smooth reach was not so much
the view, even at night, when the far banks
glittered with tiny lights, as the sound
the tires made on its steel-grid deck. I called it
"the singing bridge." If I felt the car
shimmy, I never imagined it was hard to control.

Later I learned that the wide water
was the Housatonic River nearing its delta,
that my "singing bridge" was named
the Sikorsky Memorial Bridge, that drivers dubbed it
"the slippery bridge." Later I came
to dread driving across it—the struggle to keep
the car in its lane—and to miss

my child-delight in the music
of rubber treads rolling on a steel grid, to miss as well
the wooden percussion that had often
frightened me almost into a run, but had become
in memory a curious comfort.

Martins Ferry

Don Colburn

If this were a letter to James Wright,
I would tell him how the rain colored everything
in its own image and how the road into town,
like the tracks and the river alongside,
is still the road out of town. I'd mention
they've renamed it for Lou "The Toe" Groza,
who made a living kicking for the Browns,
and how it still goes past the hobo jungle
and the dark red barns of Wheeling-Pittsburgh steel,
how the bridge arcs its black latticework
above the river.

In the old high school auditorium—
hard seats, halflight, a purple curtain
hiding the basketball court—
the poets on stage are talking about rivers,
not just the Ohio a few streets east,
but all the rivers they have gathered at:
Monongahela, Delaware, Hudson, Iowa, Styx.
For they know a river leads back to the past
and down to the sea, all that lovely corruption
and a far shore.
                    Ten years,
and we're still dredging metaphor
out of that river. This morning's paper
hollers "RIVER YIELDS BOUND BODY"
above a gaudy photo of pink dogwood.

Yields, as if the Ohio gave it up,
the body a hostage or a harvest.
A barge worker found it upriver near the dam,
tied like a calf. No one knows.

From the high school steps you can still see
all the way to the river and Terminal Bridge
and downstream to the blue gap
where sky divides the hills, two states.
Even from here a river changes the world.
I want to tell James Wright
the Ohio's pretty much the same,
still on its way to Wheeling,
watering down what men do to it.
Tired, necessary beauty,
it keeps on toward us and away.

A Bridge

Pham Tien Duat

Father, you sent me a photo of a bridge
you built across the deep river. You say
the train will soon pass by. Show your mother
this picture. Let her keep it a good long time.

I love bridges. The spider with his web builds a small bridge
across the sweet mouth of the water jar. The magpie flies
and builds a bridge of wind across the riverbank.
The ant, crossing the canal, makes a bridge of bamboo leaves.

I love a rainbow when the wind rises and the rainbow
becomes a bridge of blue and red streaks in the sky.
Under the rainbow bridge, a factory has just been built,
its smoke whiter than clouds before rain.

I love the bamboo bridge over the canal where I stand
waiting for my mother at rice harvest. I love to watch
the women carry rice on their hardened shoulders,
turning the waters yellow under the bridge.

I love the suspension bridge near my grandmother's house.
The bridge is a hammock slung over the river, rocking people
side to side. Under the bridge, boats carry lime and gravel,
sails push against the current, small thin barks glide down.

But what I love most, even more than the bridge by the pond
where my mother bends to soak beans is the bridge in this photo.
My mother says, "It's Ham Rong Bridge across Ma River."
But I call it my father's bridge.

1964

These Miles to My River

NANCY FLYNN

I set off in shoes that pinch,
sink heel deep in the mud across levees
to worship at the street of Erato,
her bridge the span of a prayer.

Beyond this archipelago of anthracite,
the miles to my river drain shorelines,
turn oxbow-weighty, the trees on the bank
sing a chorus of umlauts and howls.

I was told there's a furnace, one smithy's forge
near the dock for the ferry where words
heated then hammered, emerge perfect,
first violin in a string quartet.

If I chew this taffy long enough,
the flavor will rise, anise India ink,
and I can float my message downstream
on the back of a leaf in a bottle:

These miles to my river wear a tragedy
of donkeys, blinkered and chained
to an underground pen.

Maneuvers
Cecelia Hagen

Walking across the footbridge
I meet a troop of soldiers
dogtrotting the other way.
Their camouflage blends them
on this concrete arch.
Each back carries a full pack,
each black boot comes down hard.

The pairs of them part around me
and there's almost laughter, though no one
laughs. This is their show of respect
and mine of modesty; their time on duty,
and my duty not to exert
the power of my singularity
by looking any one of them in the eye.

In the military town I grew up in,
girls learned to ignore the catcalls
of soldiers and sailors,
pretend they didn't hear
the wolf whistles or the sly
Hey baby, want a ride?

Girls learned to move the way this river does,
completely other, contained, oblivious.
This cool reserve has become

my own black boot, my pack, my camouflage.
Now the soldiers are cresting the bridge,
nearly through with this maneuver.
Their trot picks up speed as if their legs
all belonged to the same eager animal.
I, too, move faster, walking down
to my destination on the opposite shore.

The bridge flexes and contracts
with the weight of our passing
while the river thinks of no one,
nothing, choosing not to.

Elsie

Marilyn Johnston

She found me lost in the woods, my brothers long since home,
watching *The Three Stooges* on our skinny-legged TV.
Earlier that day I'd followed them while they hunted
Confederate minnie balls down by the Appomattox Bridge,
water licking our bare feet. I didn't think she'd come—
the sapping heat, the mosquitoes and poison ivy,
the cloying din of gnats and flies around my ears,
saying *alone again* as I crouched beside a blackberry thicket
near the bend in the river. It was late afternoon,
shadows folding out of sycamore trees, when I finally
heard my name—Elsie, our maid, shouting
Mar-i-lyn! Where are you, child?
rounding up her charge, guiding me home.

The next day we rode together on the city bus and Elsie
waited while I took three big steps down onto the sidewalk
in front of Flora M. Hill Elementary,
waited while I entered the door of first grade.
She was standing at the school's front door as the last bell rung.
We sat in the rear of the bus, holding hands, her dark palms
around my pale fingers as we looked out over
the Appomattox Bridge toward Elsie's side of town,
heard how the driver talked to the Coloreds who dared
enter by the front bus door, dared to take a seat behind him.
I told Elsie I'd never want to sit up there, that I'd stay
with her in the back as long as she needed—and I'd find her,
even if she was lost in the woods in the middle of the night
in a poison ivy patch, *pinky swear I would*.

Moon-Set

DOROTHY BLACKCROW MACK

Nothing left but rocks   sea and sky
  I set my course on you

  each clear night
  as you toss your shimmering band
  down onto the water
  you whisper
      reach   *catch me*

how can I stretch my desolate arms
up to you, so high and pale
no water wings to swim the air
no flippers to fly the waves
how I can walk on water

if I make silver slippers
to slide on your ribbon
to the edge of the sea
still I cannot reach you
how can I climb on air

  each clear night
  as you toss your shimmering band
  down onto the waves
  you whisper
      reach   *catch me*

I wait till you grow fat and lustrous
dropping down to rebirth yourself
in the black waters of the night horizon

and as you drop I catch you
midwife you
as you midwife me

Caroling

JOSEPH MILLAR

We clutched the purple mimeos
of Joy to the World and God Rest Ye Merry
as we sang a cappella, a bit out of time,
next to the fly-speckled angel
in the La Honda Home for the Aged.

The patients sat up straight in their pj's
under the fragrant pine boughs,
wheezed, giggled, clapped and waved.
And my brother walked out among them
bending down in his white shirt
to listen, nodding, giving away
the tissue-wrapped navel oranges.
Later he'd lead me to two old men
lying in neighboring beds, rough
faces deepened by weather,
big hands fleshy and scarred.
Clarence and Dale from North Dakota,
brothers who'd followed the wheat harvest,
picked apples together in Washington state.
Sometimes they need extra oxygen
and both of them suffer bad knees and feet—
smiling broadly, without many teeth
after ninety-one Christmases.

Don't ask me why I've waited here
locked up inside the hours and years
or why I keep turning away.
Don't ask me why I wake up so early
and stand on the bridge before work
watching red leaves drift into the river
and thinking nothing will last.

Heaven of the Moment
John Morrison

Our love would be enough as long as we
never left the county by the highway north
to Montgomery and across the bridge arched
over the muddy Tombigbee. She
feared falling, how the high arc might buckle
like flimsy tin and our car tumble
to the alligator roil in the swamp below.

My problem was the sky. The span aimed us
to whatever weather was there: plump,
lazy thunderheads, hazy sunshine, heavy rain,
or night and stars that seethed as we
came closer. Gravity could forget to keep
our tires tight to the road and the ramp
would fling us into the heaven of the moment
where she and I were sure to let go.

Ghost Bridge

BILL SIVERLY

Summer nights my father drove us in his pride,
A fifty-three Buick Special heavy with chrome and steel,
Clattering over the rickety Eighteenth Street Bridge
That spanned the Clearwater River to North Lewiston,
To see movies at the drive-in, like *Destination Moon*.

Built in nineteen-thirteen, Eighteenth Street Bridge
Put Silcott's downstream cable ferry out of business,
After fifty years of service from the founding of the town.
In the nineteen twenties Clarence would ride his horse with no
Saddle from the ranch at the foot of Lewiston Hill,

Across the Eighteenth Street Bridge up Normal Hill to school.
North Lewiston forever the wrong side of the river—
To come from there, by horse no less, shows lack of class.
You surely must have shit on your shoes, Hayseed,
Surely you will spend the rest of your life in this town.

Just before the south end of the Eighteenth Street Bridge
Stood a small white cinderblock café called Jack's Place.
Six a.m., my father and I on our way upriver would park the Buick,
Meet Clarence among the mumbling mill-hands and fishermen,
The air thick with bacon, coffee, tobacco, and damp flannel.

By nineteen fifty-eight the Eighteenth Street Bridge was gone,
Replaced by Clearwater Memorial Bridge upstream.
Today the Army Corps has reconfigured the levee, and Jack's Place
Exists no more. Whenever I swing by, I want to turn,
As if to cross again that bridge to destinations yet unknown.

Our Story

WILLIAM STAFFORD

Remind me again—together we
trace our strange journey, find
each other, come on laughing.
Sometime we'll cross where life
ends. We'll both look back
as far as forever, that first day.
I'll touch you—a new world then.
Stars will move a different way.
We'll both end. We'll both begin.

Remind me again

Assignment
ANN STALEY

It's sizzling outside and 83 degrees inside
as I plan for upcoming classes,
compose an essay,
and here comes my friend's September reminder:
a poem about bridges.
The Bridge to Terabithia
The Bridge on the River Kwai
The Bridge to Nowhere
A Bridge Too Far.
Then I remember Foster Street—
how it ran east to west,
past the Department of Health and Human Services
and the museum where I first saw Andrew Wyeth's paintings;
past the crisis hot line where I volunteered one winter,
past red brick row houses becoming the hood
right on to the shores of the Susquehanna River,
and across to the island where the B leagues played baseball,
and the poor families picnicked,
where the annual July fireworks were staged,
the starting point for a swimming meet I participated in one summer.
Then across the wide, undulant river to the west side of the city
where the country club had black caddies, cooks, and servers—
good jobs—but no black members.
The Foster Street Bridge cut through all of my childhood,
and an industrial city become suburban state capitol.
On it my eyes opened to civil rights and protest, athletics and art.
I remember it now, across the continent, itself a bridge
between my two lives.

Twists and Turns
Debbie West

There are many
twists and turns
in the heart.
Locked doors,
secret passages.

There was a fault line
going all the way through
my heart.
One day something moved
deep inside me,
and ripped it open,
splitting us apart.

The entire landscape of my life
changed
in a few short sentences.

No matter how we tried after that,
and we did try,
we couldn't bridge the rift
that divided us.

Song For Us All

JUDITH BARRINGTON

Where the water runs through the canyon
where the sagebrush is smoky blue,
there the soldiers were far too many—
there Chief Joseph's men were few.

And did the people build a bridge?
And did the people plant a seed?
Was there friendship across the water?
And did a rose grow among the weeds? (repeat)

Under pine trees and sweet magnolias,
by the ocean and mountain stream,
we were divided, slave and master,
until we fastened upon a dream.

And did the people build a bridge?
And did the people plant a seed?
Was there friendship across the water?
And did a rose grow among the weeds? (repeat)

Like the desert and the cornfields
we were different all along—
some could stand and some could see,
some could hear the blackbird's song.

And did the people build a bridge?
And did the people plant a seed?
Was there friendship across the water?
And did a rose grow among the weeds? (repeat)

Now we are one and we are many
reaching out to those who fear.
If we live with love, however we choose,
the waters between us will run clear.

And we the people build the bridge.
And we the people plant the seeds.
There is friendship across the water.
There are roses as well as weeds. (repeat)

Contributors' Notes

Mark Alter is a retired social worker and community organizer. His poems, a play, a memoir, and many articles and letters have been influenced by visits to Japan. He lives within walking distance of the 1905 hanging deck truss that carries Thurman Street over Balch Gulch in Northwest Portland.

Judith Arcana's poems, stories, and essays have been published in journals and anthologies for more than 30 years. Her most recent book is the poetry collection *What if your mother*; among her prose books is *Grace Paley's Life Stories, A Literary Biography*. Raised in Chicago, she now lives in Northeast Portland and is on-line at <www.juditharcana.com>.

Elizabeth Archers is coeditor of two volumes of open-mic poetry anthologies and has published four small "chaplets" of her work, *Blood, Junk, Age,* and *Love,* to be combined in a single chapbook, *Full of Myself* (forthcoming). She hosts a monthly salon, The Church of Poetry, in her Portland home. Her favorite bridge is the Headless Horseman Bridge from *The Legend of Sleepy Hollow*.

Mary Barnard (1909–2001), a graduate of Reed College who lived mostly in Vancouver, Washington, won *Poetry* magazine's Levinson Award in 1935. Her

Sappho: A New Translation, published in 1958, has sold more than 100,000 copies and remains in print. *Collected Poems*, with an introduction by William Stafford, was published in 1979 and won the Elliston Award. She won, at age 77, the 1986 Western States Book Award for Poetry, for *Time and the White Tigress*, a verse-essay bridging art and science.

Judith Barrington is the author of three volumes of poetry, most recently *Horses and the Human Soul*. *Lifesaving: A Memoir* won the Lambda Book Award in 2000 and was a finalist for a PEN/Martha Albrand Award and an Oregon Book Award. She teaches writing in the U.S., Britain, and Spain. Her Web site is <www.judithbarrington.com>.

Eleanor Berry's book of poems, *Green November*, was published by Traprock Books in 2007. Her poems have appeared in *Crab Orchard Review, Dogwood, Nimrod*, and *Windfall*, and are forthcoming in *Prairie Schooner*. A recent essay on the poetry of Lorine Niedecker is included in *Reading the Middle Generation Anew* (University of Iowa Press, 2006). Her favorite bridge is the Brooklyn Bridge, in part because of Marianne Moore's poem "Granite and Steel," and in part because of seeing it at dawn 40 years ago with her husband of 39 years, Richard Berry.

Jonah Bornstein, coauthor of *A Path Through Stone*, was nominated for a Pushcart Prize in 2000 for his poem "Night Blooming Men." He has been published in the anthologies *September 11, 2001: American Writers Respond; Deer Drink the Moon: Poems of Oregon*; and *Intricate Homeland*. He lives in Ashland, Oregon.

Josephine Bridges has published a collection of 12 poetry postcards and a book of poetry, *The Only Word There Is (you guess which one)*. Her second poetry collection, *Congratulations and Condolences*, is awaiting publication, and she's finishing up a third book of poetry, *Tornado Hits Trailer Park*. A freelance writer and teacher of English as a Foreign Language, she is developing a plan to live in 20 countries in 20 years. The editors of this book admire her name.

Robert Cohen's first poetry collection, *Talking Back to the Moon*, was published in 2005 by Traprock Books. He once lived, and later worked, in a homeless shelter sited under the east end of the Hawthorne Bridge. He now lives in Coos Bay, Oregon.

Don Colburn, formerly with *The Washington Post*, now reports for *The Oregonian*. He has been a finalist for the Pulitzer Prize for feature writing. His poetry chapbook, *Another Way to Begin*, won the Finishing Line Press Prize in 2006. A full-length collection, *As If Gravity Were a Theory*, won the Cider Press Review Book Award, also in 2006. He is a board member of the Friends of William Stafford. His favorite bridge is the one that will get him across to wherever he's going. He's at <www.doncolburn.net>.

Walt Curtis cofounded the Oregon Cultural Heritage Commission and is the cohost, with Barbara LaMorticella, of Talking Earth, a poetry program broadcast by Portland's KBOO Community Radio. Poet, historian, essayist, and artist, he is known as Portland's Unofficial Poet Laureate. His autobiographical *Mala Noche* (Bad Night) inspired Gus Van Sant's first film, released in 1985. His favorite bridge is the Steel Bridge, for its "stunning" black industrial look.

Brian Doyle is the editor of *Portland Magazine* at the University of Portland, and the author of eight books of essays and "proems," most recently *Epiphanies & Elegies*. His work has appeared in *The Best American Essays*, *Best Spiritual Writing*, and *Best Science and Nature Writing* anthologies. His favorite bridge is the Summer Street Bridge in Boston, where he "savored a loooong lovely kiss there once with a brief lovely woman."

Pham Tien Duat is one of the most respected poets in Vietnam. He served as a soldier and poet along the Ho Chi Minh Trail for ten years during the war and has published multiple collections of poetry.

Stephen Dunn's first book of poems, *Five Impersonations*, was published in 1971. He has published 16 books of poetry over the course of his career, most recently *Different Hours*, for which he won the Pulitzer Prize in 2001. He lives in western Maryland.

Ed Edmo, poet, performer, traditional storyteller, and lecturer on Northwest tribal culture, is a consultant to the Smithsonian's National Museum of the American Indian and recipient of a National Endowment for the Arts grant. His poetry, short stories, and plays have been widely published. His favorite bridge is the Burnside Bridge, a bridge over which, he writes, he now walks sober.

Jean Esteve, a painter and writer living in Waldport, Oregon, is one of the earliest members of the long-established Tuesday writing group that meets weekly in Waldport. Her poems have been published in *Poetry Daily, Iowa Review, Mudfish*, and the *Harvard Review*. Her favorite bridge is the Alsea Bay Bridge. "Dogs," she writes, "don't need leashes when we walk across it."

Nancy Flynn grew up on the Susquehanna River in the anthracite coal region of northeastern Pennsylvania. She recently moved to Portland after nine years living in the Coast Range woods near Corvallis. She is a recipient of a 2004 Oregon Literary Fellowship. Her chapbook, *The Hours of Us*, is forthcoming from Finishing Line Press. Her Web site is <www.nancyflynn.com>.

C.A. Gilbert lives in Florence, Oregon. His poetry chapbooks include *Portage* and a collaborative effort, with Erik Muller, *Lakes*. He is a senior advisor for a national financial services firm. The first magnificent bridge he can recall is the Golden Gate, the bridge of his youth.

Ruth Harrison, of Waldport, Oregon, is a retired professor of medieval literature. Her poetry has appeared in regional, national, and international quarterlies and journals and her collections include *Bone Flute* (1996) and *Namesong* (2004). Two chapbooks are carried in Oregon coast bookstores. Her favorite bridge is the Crooked Wash Bridge, a suspension bridge over a turbulent stream near Elk Springs, Colorado. She remembers watching her father cross it safely in high wind when she was four years old.

Cecelia Hagen grew up in Norfolk, Virginia. Portland's 26 Books Press published her chapbook *Fringe Living*. She's been awarded fellowships from Soapstone, the MacDowell Colony, and Caldera, and a writing grant from Literary Arts. The *Passager Journal*, published by the University of Baltimore, chose her as the 2007 Passager Poet. She loves crossing the car-free DeFazio Bridge over the Willamette River in Eugene.

Seamus Heaney, born in Ireland, won the Nobel Prize in Literature in 1995 for what the Nobel committee described as "works of lyrical beauty and ethical depth." His latest book of poetry, *District and Circle*, won the 2006 T.S. Eliot Prize. He lectured at the Arlene Schnitzer Concert Hall as part of the Portland Arts & Lectures 2002–2003 series. His poem "Scaffolding" was written for his wife, the writer Marie Devlin Heaney.

Donna Henderson's poems, reviews, and essays have appeared in literary journals, anthologies, public art installations, performance venues, and two chapbook collections. She is a psychotherapist by profession, a founding member of the piano and poetry performance ensemble Tonepoem, and holds an MFA in creative writing from Warren Wilson College. "My new best friend," she writes, "is definitely the Morrison Bridge, having gotten to watch it open its arms from underneath this past July."

Diane Holland is a painter, printmaker, teacher, and poet. Her first collection, *The Hand Stayed From Its Desire*, won the 2006 Predator Press chapbook prize and was nominated for a Pushcart Prize. Her poems have also appeared in many literary journals. She divides her time between Oregon and Alaska. She admires the Hawthorne Bridge. "It's honest, sturdy, yet eloquent architecture. I love that it is what it is."

Lawson Inada is the Oregon Poet Laureate. He is the author of five books and the editor of three, including *Only What We Could Carry: The Japanese American Internment Experience*. He won the American Book Award in 1994 for *Legends from Camp*. From the Houghton Mifflin Web site: "His poetics of performance posits his art not as an object that transcends time but as a process that shapes time." This laureate's favorite bridge is the handshake. He lives in Medford, Oregon with his wife, Janet Inada.

David Johnson (1945–2006) lived and worked, primarily as a journalist, in several cities and towns in Oregon as well as Chicago, the Bay Area, and during 2001–2003, Blagoveshchensk, Russia. His publications include a natural history of the tufted puffin, published by the Bandon Historical Society, for which he also did letterpress printing. His is one of the three interweaving voices in the poetry collection *Confluence*, which was a finalist for the 1993 Oregon Book Award. *Pitching My Tent on Slanted Ground* was published in 2005. He lived in St. Johns at the time of his death.

Marilyn Johnston has been published in many journals and anthologies. She received the Donna Stone National Literary Award, a Robert Penn Warren

Award, and writing fellowships from Oregon Literary Arts, Fishtrap, and the Barbara Deming Fund. The Habit of Rainy Nights Press published her chapbook, *Red Dust Rising*, in 2004. Born in Richmond, Virginia, she grew up by the Appomattox River Bridge.

Ted Kooser is the author of ten books of poems, two collections of nonfiction, and numerous chapbooks. He served as the National Poet Laureate of the United States between 2004 and 2006, and received the Pulitzer Prize in Poetry for *Delights and Shadows* in 2005. He lives in Nebraska.

Sarah Lantz (1958–2007) was published by *CALYX Journal, The Denver Quarterly, Paris Atlantic*, and *Margie,* among others. She taught Poetry in the Schools in Oregon (through Literary Arts) and in Hawaii (through a National Endowment for the Arts grant). She was a featured poet on National Public Radio's *Morning Edition*, and on Canadian Broadcasting's equivalent, for her translations of Nushu, an ancient form of poetry created by women in Hunan, China, to record their autobiographies.

Dorianne Laux's latest book is *Facts about the Moon* (W.W. Norton), recipient of the 2006 Oregon Book Award. She teaches at the University of Oregon and in Pacific University's low-residency MFA program. She lives in Eugene with her husband, the poet Joseph Millar. "There is something about the strength and delicacy of bridges, the impossibility of them," she writes. Her favorite bridge is the Astoria-Megler Bridge, where she has watched big barges glide under it in the rain.

Dorothy Blackcrow Mack's poem "Wind Ave II: Time of Emergence" was nominated for a Pushcart Prize. She directs Willamette Writers Coast Branch, teaches at Oregon Coast Community College, and leads creative nonfiction workshops. She is writing a memoir, *Belonging to the Black Crows*, and a mystery set on a reservation, *The Handless Maiden*. Her favorite bridge is "most powerful, most universal—Bridge Between Worlds."

Melissa Madenski has taught at the Northwest Writing Institute, Sitka Center, and in public and private schools. Her essays and poems have appeared regionally and nationally. She is Writer in Residence at Arbor School of Arts and Science in Tualatin, Oregon. She writes that she has always loved and will always love rivers and the bridges that cross them.

Morton Marcus has published ten volumes of poetry and one novel, most recently *Moments Without Names: New & Selected Prose Poems* and *Pursuing the Dream Bone*. His poems have appeared in over 85 anthologies, and he has read his work and taught creative writing workshops at universities throughout the U.S. and Europe. His memoir, *Striking Through The Masks*, is forthcoming. He's on-line at <www.mortonmarcus.com>.

Joy McDowell writes from studios in the Willamette Valley and on the Coos Bay estuary. Her poetry, essays, and short stories have appeared in publications in New York, Texas, Washington, and Oregon. Her book of poems, *Waltzing the Dragon*, was published in 1997. Of the McCullough Bridge over Coos River at North Bend, she writes "The tides come and go twice each day—allowing for mistakes and regret to be washed away and fresh new energy to flush in—all beneath the green bridge."

Michael McDowell coedits *Windfall: A Journal of Poetry of Place*, specializing in Northwest poetry in which "place" works as an essential element of the poem. He teaches composition, literature, and creative writing at Portland Community College's Sylvania campus. He writes about the Hawthorne Bridge: "One of my favorite family stories is my grandmother's account of how in the 1910s when she was walking downtown from the east side, the lift tender let her ride high up into the air on the sidewalk as the bridge lifted to let a ship go under."

Katy McKinney lives in Trout Lake, Washington, at the foot of Mt. Adams. She has published poems in *The Sun, Manzanita Quarterly, Windfall, Pacific Magazine, Pontoon 9,* and *Not What We Expected,* an anthology of poems about motherhood. She recently received her MFA in Writing from Pacific University. She likes the Hood River Bridge because it's scenic and gets her to the grocery store.

David Memmott is the author of four poetry books and the science fiction novel *Prime Time,* published in 2007 by Wordcraft of Oregon. His poems have appeared in *Deer Drink the Moon: Poems of Oregon, Salt: A Collection of Poetry on the Oregon Coast,* and in *The High Desert Journal.* Now a resident of La Grande, he once worked in fish canneries on Astoria's waterfront. "The Astoria Bridge was always there as a reminder that the way is open to other lands, other worlds— we just need to maintain the bridges."

Joseph Millar is the author of *Fortune,* from Eastern Washington University Press. His first collection, *Overtime* (2001), was a finalist for the Oregon Book Award. His poems have appeared in many magazines and journals, including *Ploughshares* and *Prairie Schooner.* He lives in Eugene, Oregon with his wife, the poet Dorianne Laux.

Margaret Gish Miller's work has appeared in *Hipfish, Verseweavers, The Peralta Press,* and *New Millennium Writings.* Born in Palo Alto, California, and now a retired English teacher, she lives in Independence, Oregon with her husband Ronald Miller. She is a faithful attendee of the Second Sunday Series of Poetry Readings in Stayton, Oregon, a small Oregon town enlivened by irrigation canals diverting the North Santiam under low-level bridges.

Sid Miller is the founder and editor of the Portland based literary journal *Burnside Review.* He is the author of two chapbooks, and his first full-length collection, *Nixon the Piano,* is forthcoming from David Robert Books in 2008. His favorite is the Astoria-Megler Bridge, where it nears the Washington shore.

Amy Klauke Minato is author of *The Wider Lens*, published in 2004 by Ice River Press. Her poetry, published in many literary journals, has been recognized with a 2003 Oregon Literary Fellowship. She teaches English at Washington State University Vancouver and poetry through Literary Arts and in other venues. She writes that she loves to lie down on a narrow footbridge over the Imnaha River in eastern Oregon. "It sways deliciously and is surrounded by sculpted cliffs."

Ada Molinoff writes to bridge the cultures of East Coast and West, and to link her practice of psychology with poetry. Her poems have appeared in *Fireweed, Riven, Jewish Women's Literary Annual, Where We Find Ourselves: Jewish Women Around the World Write About Home*, and in the four chapbooks published by the Peregrine Writers Group. She lives in Salem. She has two favorite land bridges and favors "any words that form a bridge between people and cultures."

Judith Montgomery lives in Bend and took her first poetry workshop in 1995. Her poetry and prose look at the questions of time, passion, sacrifice, and duty, especially in the developing lives of women. Her chapbook, *Passion*, was awarded the 2000 Oregon Book Award. *Red Jess*, her first full-length collection, was published in 2006, and *Pulse & Constellation* was a finalist for the Finishing Line Press Chapbook Competition in 2007. She best loves the Fremont's "glorious arch."

John Morrison received the 2004 C. Hamilton Bailey Poetry Fellowship from Literary Arts. His poems have appeared in many journals including *Natural Bridge*. He teaches poetry at Washington State University Vancouver. "Heaven of the Moment" is the title poem of his first collection of poetry, published in 2007 by Bedbug Books. His favorite bridge is the Honey Run Covered Bridge across Butte Creek. "We used to walk through the cool of the bridge to inner tube down the creek. I remember water, shadow, wood, and a route of secret passage into the heat of an early afternoon."

Erik Muller, of Eugene, is the publisher of Traprock Books and a critic of Western poetry. His essays are part of the Western Writers Series from Boise State University. *Northwest Review* published his essays on Richard Dankleff, Barbara Drake, and Kenneth Hanson in 2006. Of the bridges the Forest Service builds over waters like Skookum Creek, he writes, "They are made to fit in and constructed of available forest wood in an absolutely transparent manner so I can see the engineering/woodcrafting!"

Erin Ocon teaches seventh- and eighth-grade language arts at R.A. Brown Middle School in Hillsboro. In addition to writing fiction and poetry, she writes about education, recently contributing to Choice Literacy <www.choiceliteracy.com>. Born in Wisconsin, she now lives in Northwest Portland, and loves the Broadway Bridge for its unique color and the way her bicycle takes to it.

Susan Parker has been writing poetry for 40 years and has been published in the Northwest journals *Luckiamute*, *The Crab Creek Review*, *Between The Lines* and other literary journals. Of "The Briefest Bridge," she writes, "My sons and I discovered this bridge in McMinnville when we lost my husband."

Paulann Petersen's books of poetry are *The Wild Awake* (Confluence Press), *Blood-Silk* (Quiet Lion Press), and *A Bride of Narrow Escape* (Cloudbank Books), which was a finalist for the Oregon Book Award. A former Stegner Fellow at Stanford University and the recipient of the 2006 Holbrook Award from Literary Arts, she serves on the board of the Friends of William Stafford as organizer for the annual Stafford Birthday events. She loves the Sellwood Bridge "for its ethereal (and now ephemeral!) beauty."

Rita Ott Ramstad teaches English at The Center for Advanced Learning, a public charter school in Gresham, and lives in Brightwood, near the foot of Mt. Hood. Her work has appeared in the Poetry in Motion program, and her first book of poetry, *The Play of Dark and Light*, won the 2003 Stafford/Hall Award for Poetry. Her favorite bridge is the Hood Canal Bridge. "Because on one side of the bridge the water is always choppy and on the other side it is smooth, and I don't know why this is, but it seems symbolic and right. Also when I cross that bridge (going west), I feel as if I'm going home."

Carlos Reyes's latest book of poems is *At the Edge of the Western Wave* (Lost Horse Press, 2004), and he is now at work on the manuscript of his "new and selected poems." His two favorite bridges are the Hoffstadt Creek Bridge (Mount St. Helens), and the Inter-American Highway Bridge (Republic of Panama). He had a part in the former's on-the-ground surveying and engineering. His grandchildren call it "Grandpa Carlos's Bridge." The latter connects South and North America, and his past with his present. He lives in Southeast Portland with his wife, book designer Karen Checkoway.

Willa Schneberg is the author of three books of poetry, including *Storytelling in Cambodia* (2006). She received the Oregon Book Award for her second collection, *In The Margins Of The World*. Garrison Keillor read one of her poems on *The Writer's Almanac,* and she recently read at the Library of Congress. A Brooklyn native, her favorite bridge is the Brooklyn Bridge. She lives in Southwest Portland, not far from the St. Johns Bridge, designed by engineer David Steinman, who remodeled the Brooklyn Bridge in 1948.

Peter Sears is the author of two books of poetry, two books on teaching poetry, and four chapbooks. His poems have appeared in *The Atlantic, Field,* and *Saturday Review.* He teaches in the low-residency MFA writing program at Pacific University and for Community of Writers. He founded the Oregon Literary Coalition and cofounded the Friends of William Stafford. He lives in Corvallis. His favorite bridge is the Sellwood Bridge, for the sign "Men Below Please Don't Throw."

Bill Siverly was born and grew up in Lewiston, Idaho, and has lived in Portland since 1972. He has published three books of poems: *Parzival* (1981), *Phoenix Fire* (1987), and *The Turn* (2000). He's taught literature, composition, and creative writing at Portland Community College for 25 years. Since 2002 he has been coeditor of *Windfall: A Journal of Poetry of Place*. His favorite bridge is the St. Johns, "for its soaring Gothic architecture!"

Joseph A. Soldati has been published in many literary journals, including *Across the Long Bridge.* He is the author of a chapbook, *Apocalypse Clam* (2006); a scholarly book, *Configurations of Faust* (1980); a poetry collection, *Making My Name* (1990). His favorite bridge is the Steel Bridge "because it resembles the great early bridges of this country, and because it's black and offers Portland's most imposing silhouette at dawn and dusk."

Douglas Spangle, poet, reviewer, editor, translator, and reader of poetry, has worked on a group of poems about Portland bridges for 20 of the last 30 years. He read his St. Johns Bridge poem, excerpted here, at the bridge's 60th anniversary rededication in 1991. It appeared in its entirety in the 26 Books chapbook *2 ½ Bridges*, published in 1999. His favorite bridge is the St. Johns Bridge, "because it's so awesome."

William Stafford (1914–1993), of mostly Kansas and Oregon, was a witness for peace and for honesty. He was the author of more than 50 books, and recipient of the National Book Award for *Traveling Through the Dark* in 1963. He served as a conscientious objector during World War II, Consultant in Poetry to the Library of Congress in 1970, and Oregon Poet Laureate 1975 to 1990. There is more about him at <www.williamstafford.org>.

Ann Staley lives in Corvallis. Oregon Parks & Recreation published her most recent essay, "Thirteen Ways of Looking at a Wetland." Her favorite bridges are hand-built "backwoods discoveries" like those along the Lower Rogue River Trail. She grew up in Harrisburg, Pennsylvania, a suburban capital divided by the Susquehanna River. She remembers seeing the Golden Gate Bridge for the first time in 1970, driving her VW across and back, "feeling the West become home."

David Steinman (1886–1960) was raised in the shadow of the Brooklyn Bridge. From a poor family, he became one of the most famous bridge engineers of the twentieth century, designing hundreds of bridges, among them the St. Johns Bridge, Mackinac Bridge, and the Henry Hudson Bridge. He also wrote poetry, and was the author of *I Built a Bridge and Other Poems*, published by Davidson Press, Inc. of New York City in 1955. The cover of this elegant book, about bridges everywhere, is embossed with the image of the St. Johns Bridge.

Dianne Stepp's poems have appeared in *Clackamas Literary Review, Comstock Review, CALYX, Willow Springs, The Oregonian, Portland Lights, Regrets Only,* and other journals and anthologies. She's a graduate of the Warren Wilson MFA Program for Writers. Her chapbook, *Half-Moon of Clay*, was published in 2006.

Sandra Stone's first collection of poems, *Cocktails with Breughel at the Museum Café*, was selected in the Cleveland State University annual manuscript competition. The following year it won the Oregon Book Award for Poetry. She has work forthcoming in *Southwest Review, Denver Quarterly,* and *Mid-West Quarterly,* and a featured review in *Poetry Flash/Berkeley*. She writes, "Portland is *hometown*, NE Wisteria Drive, first lamp, Burnside Bridge, first bridge, less structurally alluring, but theatrical, diverse and vocal."

Colette Tennant's poems have appeared in various journals and anthologies, most recently in *The Dos Passos Review, Global City Review's* simple virtues issue and *Natural Bridge's* dream issue. Her book, *Reading the Gothic in Margaret*

Atwood's Novels, was published in December 2003. She lives in Salem. Her favorite bridge is the Rialto Bridge in Venice. "The Rialto is so lacy and sweet and white—ready for a festival to begin at any moment."

Jack Turteltaub is an Oregon native and belongs to the Nulla Dies poetry group. His poetry has appeared in *Verseweavers, Connecticut River Review, Rosebud, Spillway,* and *Edgz,* among others. He occasionally writes for the Portland publication *Just Out,* and is in private practice as a clinical psychologist/coach. The canyons and high country of the Great Basin and the Colorado Plateau have influenced him. His favorite bridge in the world is the Golden Gate; in Portland, the Fremont.

Debbie West is a multimedia artist and writer living in Portland. She recently completed (for now) *The Book of Love, A Work in Progress,* a collage book of original artwork and poetry. Her poem "Twists and Turns" is included on *The Good Horse* CD, released in 2007 by Portland musician Paula Sinclair. West's favorite Portland bridge to look at is the St. Johns Bridge, "so beautiful it's not fair to the rest of the bridges." Her favorite to use is the Hawthorne, "because it's the best to bike over (usually)."

Victoria Fairham Wheeler is a lifelong educator. She writes fiction, nonfiction, and poetry, and has two published books for teachers, *The Positive Teacher* and *Daily Writing Topics Grades 7–12* from The Center for Learning. Her writing is influenced by growing up in and outside of Detroit, Michigan where cars shaped the culture, as well as her migration to the Northwest in 1975. She lives in Milwaukie with her husband Kevin Wheeler, an energy specialist and songwriter. Her favorite bridge is the Ambassador Bridge, connecting Detroit to Windsor, Ontario.

Doreen Gandy Wiley has been on Oregon's writing scene since the mid-sixties.

With four books of poetry, a novel, and a memoir published, she is now working on a second memoir. Retired after 17 years as an English instructor at Portland Community College, Doreen leads workshops, gives readings, and promotes poetry in Oregon. Her favorite bridge is the Steel Bridge, "for its character."

Charlie White, Distinguished (Emeritus) Professor of History, taught at Portland State University from 1952 to 2006. He was the PSU Director of International Education (1970–1985) and Director of Summer Session (1970–1989). He has a BA and an MA from Michigan State College and a PhD from the University of Southern California. Of the Mackinac Bridge on the Upper Peninsula of Michigan, he writes, "It's beautiful, it's stately, it's in my native village."

Victoria Wyttenberg taught high school for 30 years. She earned an MFA in poetry from the University of Washington in 1991 and was awarded the Richard Hugo Prize by Poetry Northwest in 1983, the Bullis-Kizer Prize in 1998, and the Academy of American Poets Prize in 1990. She is published in many literary journals and anthologies, including *From Here We Speak*. She writes of the Burnside Bridge, "It is a bridge that connects us with sadness as well as with beauty, since it forces us to acknowledge the homeless, the addicts, and the needy of our city."

Sophie Zaffina has lived in the Portland area since 1970. Her poems have appeared in many small press magazines and several anthologies. Her chapbook, *Ore*, won the Kinloch Rivers Memorial Poetry Prize in 2001. She has an MFA in Creative Writing from the University of Oregon. She works at the Old Town Clinic and lives in Southwest Portland. Her favorite bridge is the Sellwood Bridge. "It's the first bridge I remember crossing over the Willamette and the only one that still feels the same as the first time I crossed it."

Afterword, by Kirsten Rian

The Academy of American Poets says Dylan Thomas's *Do not go gentle into that good night* is the most e-mailed poem around, which I find interesting . . . we must need a voice like his from time to time, urging to continue on, bravely and fiercely, over the difficult waters of life, up to the last glimmer.

What remains, I think, are the bridges of memory, one snapshot, one remembered moment at a time, spanning back to childhood or yesterday. We all have them: these little crisscrossing arches over our history, we are built of them. In this book, 70 poets—world-renowned writers mingled with emerging voices, from the shores of Ireland to the banks of the Willamette—string their words to story. These pages are graced with bridges over frozen rivers, hearts, Celilo Falls, husbands and wives, war, peace, homelessness, suicide, school children, aging, friendship . . . and everything in between. What began as a small publication of poetry referencing Portland bridges grew to a collection evidencing the ways we keep going; how we, each in our own way, build and find the necessary bridges.

An abundance of thanks to the poets, each and every one. And to Sharon Wood Wortman, I'm still looking for words bigger than "thank you."

With gratitude,
Kirsten Rian
October, 2007

Index to Place Names

Editor's Note: Illustrations are indicated by bold italics.

Colophon

The text for *Walking Bridges Using Poetry as a Compass: Poems about Bridges Real and Imagined by 70 Poets, with Directions for Five Self-Guided Explorations* is printed on 60-pound Gray's Harbor Quinault opaque stock. The cover is printed on 12 point Tango C1S board stock finished with a 1.5 mil gloss film laminate. The display typeface is Tempus Sans ITC and the body typeface is Brioso Pro 12 point with 16 points leading. Brioso typeface was among the winners of the 2002 Type Directors Club Type Design Competition and means "lively" in Italian. Robert Slimbach designed it for Adobe Systems, Inc. in the calligraphic tradition of the Latin alphabet, modeling it on formal roman and Italian script. Tempus Sans is a standard Windows operating system typeface. The itinerary numbers and captions are Lithos Pro. The layout was created using Adobe InDesign CS3 on a Macintosh dual processor 2 GHz Power PC G5 with operating system version 10.4. The interior drawings were created with a Sakura Pigma Micron 05 pen with a 0.45 mm width line. The maps were created in Illustrator. The drawings were scanned using an Epson Stylus CX5400 flatbed scanner and Adobe Photoshop CS3.

Urban Adventure Press, founded in Portland, Oregon in 2005, published *Walking Bridges Using Poetry as a Compass*. Jennifer Omner, of ALL Publications, created the design and layout, and Jennifer Omner and Sharon Wood Wortman designed the cover from a postcard of the bridges and waterways of Portland, Oregon, also published by Urban Adventure Press. A thousand copies of *Walking Bridges Using Poetry as a Compass* were printed on a Timson offset web press and perfect bound by Bridgetown Printing Co. of Portland.